How to Flirt with a Men :

How to Flirt with Verbal Communications to Signal a Desire for Sex, Understand Men with the Art of Seduction and Sexual Intelligence

Tiffany Melara

Disclaimer

All erudition supplied in this book are specified for educational and academic purpose only. The author is not in any way in charge of any outcomes that emerge from utilizing this book. Constructive efforts have been made to render information that is both precise and effective, however, the author is not to be held answerable for the accuracy or use/misuse of this information.

Foreword

I will like to thank you for taking the very first step of trusting me and deciding to purchase/read this life-transforming book. Thanks for investing your time and resources on this product.

I can assure you of precise outcomes if you will diligently follow the specific blueprint I lay bare in the information handbook you are currently checking out. It has transformed lives, and I firmly believe it will equally change your own life too.

All the information I provided in this Do It Yourself piece is easy to absorb and practice.

CHAPTER ONE

How to Attract a Man

Making a guy fall in love with you does not look like a regular hobby, and most ladies would testify that the experience can get a little aggravating for words. Gone are the days when love seems to be something that only fate permits-- now, you can, produce tourist attraction and make that kid yours at last!

Get friendly. That's the appeal of being a girl-- getting familiar with a guy will not make him think you're hitting on him. The majority of men would most likely enjoy engaging you in a conversation. They're just programmed to respond that method with women. So go ahead, approach him, and say hi. That's a good start.

Offer tips that you're squashing on him, or if you desire to go that far, bite the bullet and tell him you like him. Liking someone does not suggest anything-- but that would surely get him a little troubled-- in an excellent method, of course!

Flirt and let him know you're interested. Read his body language. If he likes to be around you too, find out. Observe if he makes eye contact and is a bit better when you're around. Make usage of some flirting signals to get him all wondering if you're appealing him to come a bit better.

Play a little hard to get. When he appears to be getting your signal that you're interested in him, he'll likely try striking on you by now. Step back and play a little hard-to-get.

Make him make the next move. Now, it's time to wait. By getting to understand each other better, you're slowly taking him to the part where he has to say he's in love-- and will ask you to be his girlfriend.

How to Attract a Man

There's someone specific you're interested in, and you're not exactly sure what on the planet you need to do about it. Must you:

(a) Let him know?

(b) Find out if he's interested in you initially?

(c) Do great things for him so that he'll see you?

(d) Unleash your inner sex siren and use him as target practice?

(e) Agonize indecisively until he leaves your life permanently?

Of all, I want you to know that I do not criticize you for selecting any of those options. Sometimes we do not get up the guts to approach the man of our dreams, who's OK. Our painful feelings of regret will drive us to ensure we do not let a 2nd opportunity pass us by.

Every man we meet offers us an opportunity to discover the seduction style that best matches us. For some women, pulling out all the stops makes the bad male's jaw drop, while other women pull it off with flair. Some women are too sensitive to rejection to approach a guy without understanding that he has at least some level of interest in her. Other women discover it simpler to be blunt and see, at last, whether their interest is reciprocated, so that they can get on with their lives.

What I can give you are three tips for guaranteeing that you do not make a fool out of yourself in your effort to attract a man that you're interested in.

1. Don't make presumptions.

You won't understand if he's best till after you've been in a dedicated relationship with him, so do not jump to the conclusion that he's Mr. Right even if he's so attractive and so lovely and such a catch!

Incredibly few women comprehend that the perfect relationship is not composed of two complete individuals: it's made up of two imperfect people who occur to work harmoniously together.

He may be the perfect guy on paper, but that's no guarantee he'll be perfect for YOU. You have no clue what a male will resemble as a boyfriend or a partner until you've been in a dedicated relationship together for some time.

Guide clear of presumptions about what kind of couple you two would make. Today, you're just guessing that you two would be excellent together. Wait and let time inform the whole story.

2. Do not give up your power.

Time and time again, I've seen gorgeous, smart, increasingly independent women end up being doormats when they fall for the wrong guy. They believe that it is an indication of their sincere devotion when they take intoxicated calls from him, accept verbal abuse, and do cute favors that are rarely reciprocated, all the while protecting the item of their affections: "He didn't mean it." "I need to be a much better person."

When we're silly-mad in love with them, men know. They know that they can do anything, and we'll still enjoy them. As an outcome, many of them like to test the limits, simply as kids test the boundaries with their moms and dads. Some men avoid late; other men say upsetting things. Still, other men sleep around.

When a lady distributes her power in the early days of a relationship, then she should be ready to accept the consequences.

One option is to hold yourself back just enough that you stay clear-headed. If you feel yourself ending up being overwhelmed by feeling around him, so that the stars in your eyes are obscuring your vision, excuse yourself. Step outside or utilize the restroom. Remind yourself that although you're enjoying his company right now, you don't know him effectively. Stay alert for any signs that there's something "off." Take what he states on great faith; however, don't believe him blindly.

I'll leave you with a story about how one male, a confessed player who dated up to 4 women at the same time, selected the women he would seduce. In other words, women who liked him too much.

3. Do not feel embarrassed or ashamed around him.

This, you may think, is an odd idea. Why would a lady feel ashamed or embarrassed around somebody she likes?

Shyness. The feeling that she's not deserving of him. Embarrassment about the explicitness of her fantasies about him. Anxiety triggered by not understanding what she can do to make him attracted to her.

Have I gone on?

We can experience a variety of unpleasant emotions when we're in the presence of someone we like a lot. Our emotional discomfort will frequently trigger us to act in synthetically methods. For example, we might become brighter, more bubbly variations of ourselves. We may talk faster or in a higher-pitched voice than usual. We might flirt in methods that seem entirely out of character.

Most awful of all, we may avoid direct eye contact with him, since we're stressed that he'll translucent us into our hearts and find the fact.

To be your real self around the man you like, you need not to let feelings of pity or shame keep you from feeling great, realistic, and at ease around him.

Attention Women - It's OK to Show Interest!

I have a confession to make to all the women: Men are unaware of anything subliminal that you do. They are. You need to be visible to get their attention.

For any of you who have lived with a male (whether it was a sweetheart, a hubby, or a brother), this will sound familiar. As you leave your house one day, you ask a guy to clean up or clean a bit while you're gone. So what does he do? He goes to the sink, puts a few things in the dishwasher, and that's it. There are still dog hair tumbleweeds traveling in the living room flooring and laundry stacks up to the ceiling. When asked about them, he undoubtedly states, "I didn't see them."

Men need the obvious. Women need to know this, specifically when it comes to communicating their interest in men.

Many women I've coached will tell me they flirt with men all the time, but never get any reaction. When I ask what they did that they were calling "flirting," practically each will tell me they "dipped at him a couple of times," or they "smiled at him a couple of times quickly " or something similar.

These two quick smiles and second glances simply do not constitute flirting in the eyes of a guy. They are simply not apparent enough.

When many women flirt with a man, they do something they believe to be flirting, but which is the truth is something too subtle for that man to discover it. Despite that female's interest, the male will leave that scenario, thinking she didn't like him.

When I state that you require to show interest that is obvious, I am not talking about you grabbing a man and sticking your tongue down his throat as you grind up against him. What I mean by revealing interest are things like smiling a bit more or touching his arm a bit when you speak with him. I suggest that you need to use your body language to express your interest. Lean in a little when you talk to him, Flirt with him. Make fun of his jokes. Engage him in some more in-depth conversation.

If you're interested in a guy you meet, do not wait for him to ask you out. Let him know you're interested.

Not only is it alright to reveal a man you're interested in, but you need to show men you're concerned because you intend to be in control of your dating life. If you believe about it, there are only two options: you can either start to show your interest or not (or to use subtle motions which convey the same message as nothing to men).

Every single time I resolve this problem, I obtain lots of emails from women saying some variation of this: " I can't do these things. If I do, men are going to assume I'm coming onto them and also will certainly just assume I wish to copulate with them." Let me resolve this misperception so we can remove it up at last.

If you are making out with a guy in his living room, he is going to assume that both of you are merely going to have a makeout session in the living room all night. The only way men know you wish to copulate with them, also because the circumstance is if you say, "Let's be naked and go in the room." Once more, men don't pick up on nuance and the semi-obvious.

The fact is that if you men, it's OK to show some interest. We are not going to over-think or assume more regarding it than what it is. If you smile, lean in and touch their arm when you're speaking to them, they're not going to think they're going to hook-up with you right there and after that or that you intend to drag us off to bed.

All they believe is that you like them, that they can ask you out and also this can be a relationship. You need to remember this the next time your initiative is telling you that they're reading all these various other points right into every little thing you do.

Girls, take control of your dating lives by showing when you're interested. When you do, not only is it all right to do that, but we men might not be happier.

Successful Techniques of How to Be Compelling To Men

It's a usual mistake in women that being seductive to guys implies you need to do some sprucing up. The reality is, this is just a little consider the worry of being fascinating.

To be attractive, there is more you need to discuss. A man will be attracted to a lady due to how she looks and outfits. To go more than the attraction period, here are a couple of reasons you need to know.

-Wait for the right time before engaging in sex.

This is the degree where women make errors. They immediately want to make him satisfied, so he will not leave if they see a guy they are interested in. And also so, they enter into sex with a man at an onset. This doesn't keep a guy; it has the in contrast result.

At this early stage of going out, you will start to ask yourself how many people you are having sex with. Find out for as long as you can in the past having sex. Having sex with a male earlier on will certainly free him of inspirations to go after you.

-Outfit Womanly.

Take note of how you clothe if you desire men to find your alluring. Men and people generally will examine books by their looks. Do not expect him to look previous your physical examination to see the actual you. It will not be reasonable for the man.

Men are very visual, and you need to look the part for them also to discover.

This does not mean that you can't wear jeans, but ensure they are ladylike denim.

Looking good does not make him finds you appealing; it also helps with self-confidence.

And this will enable you to flirt with him favorably.

-You must flirt.

If you want him to come close, flirt with a man. You will see that a lot of men will not come near a female until they know that it's OK.

It does not have to be all teasing. It's a good idea. A lengthy and also candid eye call with a smile will do wonders.

When you smile at a guy, you offer him the environment-friendly light signal that it's OK to chat with you or ask you out. Give him several smiles forever action.

-Loving Yourself.

It raises the attraction when men see that women like themselves and their lives. The reason for this is because women that want themselves are less dependent psychologically, which is a significant turn off for men.

How to Stop Repelling Men So You Can Attract and Hold Their Attention

There is a trap women drop right into that repels men much, away. If you genuinely want to bring in a man who will add to your joy, this book shows you what pushes back men and after that gives you seven steps you can take to be extra appealing to the man you want to attract.

A young man was bragging to two women that seemed to urge him. When the door closed behind him, I heard this conversation between the two women.

" Such a wonderful kid."

" Yes, he's such a wonderful boy."

" Two things make him less appealing."

" What's that?"

"' Sweet' and 'kid.'".

" And the wedded piece sort of draws.".

I ultimately looked up from staring at the floor to take in these two girls whose words and tone about a man - likely the male who had merely been appreciating their attention - made them sound mean and unpleasant. When I checked out their faces, I saw sneers. They felt superior to the guy they were talking, and the condescension trickled them off like blood off fangs.

I assumed, "No male - no healthy man anyhow - would wish to cuddle beside that.

A man-child might, someone whose self-esteem is so harmed, he seeks condescension and punishment from the women in his life. However, no healthy and balanced male would give these two a second glimpse.".

If you wish to attract a man's interest, if you want him to find you eye-catching, the opposite of superiority is the place you intend to go. Let be clear: the opposite of supremacy is not inferiority. Instead, the reverse of prevalence is regard.

The best partnership recommendations I ever got (as well as it is an item of suggestions that life has shown right) is that men react to regard as if you hung the moon. When you admire a man, particularly if you claim, "I respect you for ___(fill in the blank) ____," you talk their language of love, and they hear it loud and clear.

Another hint: when you say it and show it, it must be valid and real both to his face and behind his back

Years ago, female recommendations masters repainted the photo of respect as a guy's language of love in terms of manipulation and satisfying the "fragile male vanity." We, women, were meant to use the information to accomplish things like getting a man in the first place, then keeping the peace, getting what you want, as well as helping love expand. In truth, that comes close to is simply an additional taste of women feeling above men, connecting concerning them in buying terms and tone while setting you up to be a manipulator.

--Valuing a guy isn't about securing a weak ego. The excellent results that include valuing a man concern how men are wired differently from women - neither better than nor much less than, just different. Valuing this distinction and appreciating a guy involves love - the exact thing.

The more regard you have for men in general and the men in your life specifically, the much more appealing you end up being to the contrary sex. Below are seven tips for how to grow regard for the men (or the man) in your life.

--Regard him behind his back.

If your friends are ill-mannered of their men in speech and tone, do not be involved.

--Look for ways to regard as well as admire. Anything will do. From the way, he wears his clothing to how he talks to others, how he handles his service, how he interacts with his friend, what his preferred foods are, what his favorite songs are, the pastimes he has, how he treats strangers, the elderly, and youngsters, etc. And keep in mind that we often tend to respect and admire people that have talents and goals that we don't share. You do not need him to be like you to respect him. Respect what's different about him. His rate of interests is different and is his own, regarding that. Or he wants to be like his daddy, respect that. He reviews the paper every morning or evening, respect that. He scents different from you, manages food differently than you, enjoys movies, and also tv programs that are not your favorite - respect everything about him.

--Regard the truth that when you have trouble, he intends to fix it.

He wants to fix your problems if you are in his circle of treatment and problem. You may not always want his help, but respect the fact that he wants to help.

--Respect the choices he makes.

Quit it if you are in the habit of going right into a power battle with him. Determine precisely how to pay attention without fighting with him.

--Respect him with your body language.

Examine the eye huffing, puffing and rolling, head shaking, silent treatment, stomping away, banging doors and drawers, and a similar task at the middle school door that lives inside you and imitate a grownup that treats herself and also others with dignity.

Whenever you can, no matter how stilted it feels, tell him what you respect him for with genuineness. When you value or appreciate him, speak it out loud to him.

Put these seven steps into practice, even as an experiment, as well as enjoy how the men in your life react to you differently. When a guy locates you appealing, he is kicked back in your presence as well as desires to invest time with you.

CHAPTER TWO

Learn how to Flirt like a Pro

Is there any type of unique means that you can flirt to make more progress with your date? From the time that we are children, we flirt with men to get what we desire. As women expand up, nevertheless, there comes to be a new strategy to flirting, and this is what you need to know.

Before you discover how to flirt to get the guy you want, you need to go over what you currently know. This is one of the most subconscious and natural ways to flirt.

One more thing you probably do when you're flirting with a guy is to grin at him. This is another extremely reliable way to get a guy's interest.

Maybe you attempt to touch him when you're flirting, which's OK. Touch is an excellent way to stimulate something between the two of you.

Do You Know How to Flirt Effectively?

OK, so you understand how to flirt, but do you know exactly how to flirt to ensure that it seems attractive and natural? We've all seen that lady at bench or club that teases in such a way that looks fake and excessively remarkable. She throws her hair back a little excessive, touches her friends a little frequently as well as laughs so loudly that you can hear her over the music. She looks absurd, but is she doing something, right? You need to know how to flirt enough to get him interested when you are teasing with a male.

o When you flirt with your eyes, you need to make eye call, but keep your gaze soft. Think seductive. You don't want to be staring your date down, as this may make him worried. Instead, punctuate your discussion with a direct gaze that smolders. When you've got it down, you'll know it.

O Flirting with touch can be very useful if you know how to do it. Do not make it look like an accident; don't make it appear to be too prepared, either.

o Smiling when you flirt is essential, but you need to know when and what kind of smile to use. If you're poking fun at something he says, then a huge smile is in order, yet if your smile is in action to a compliment, perhaps a softer fifty percent smile will make him swoon. Frequently, it's a great idea to allow your face to do the talking since our smile reflects the situation typically.

It's not hard to flirt the appropriate means once you are aware of the know-how. Given that knowing how to flirt is acquired behavior in many ways, it's an issue of stepping up your video game to get what you want.

Learn to Flirt Like a Pro - Get Out of the Corner and Put Yourself in the Game

Do you need to learn to flirt to ensure that you can boost your dating life? Would certainly you such as to be a woman who is the focal point for a change? Can you improve your social experience with some teasing tips? Continue reading, and learn to flirt like an expert.

-Deal with yourself. Place your best foot ahead before you also step out of the door to go out in the evening. Maintain yourself healthy with a proper diet and workout. There is more to living healthy than looking excellent.

You will be more confident when you are meeting people when you take proper care of yourself. You feel great, and you look excellent. You do not need to work out like a movie celebrity, but if you are in a suitable shape, you'll be your ideal self.

Make sure that there is more to your time than simply work and residence. This may seem like it has nothing to do with how to flirt, but in truth, it is an important trick.

The best flirts more than happy, confident people with active lives and minds. If you regularly want to meet on your own, then you will be a much appealing person to be around. You will have exciting stories to tell, at least.

You might want to meet a man, but have you ever asked yourself if you like men? You will certainly not be an effective flirt with this perspective!

Keep in mind that men share the same thoughts and feeling that women do. We are not all the same, which's a great thing. Vive la distinction! That does not mean that you can't relate to people at all.

Some women appear to be born with the ability to attract men. But, even if you're not one of those women, you can learn to flirt with ease and confidence.

Dating Fun: Schedule a Date Like a Pro

Scheduling enjoyable dates appear to have to be progressively harder for the women I train on how to have dating enjoyable. One of the reoccurring questions I am asked is, "how do I get my days scheduled with less problem and more ease"?

If a guy is much more hesitant than you prepared for about setting up a date, it is not necessarily a red flag. Your role is to break this hesitation smoothly - a little teasing ought to do the method. Here are five tips you can apply to have your male sitting next to you on your next fun date.

- Go into your date "scheduling discussion" with a feasible plan for a suitable partner. Casually move the discussion to talk about available dates. If he appears not capable of using a tip for a date; but, you will have an enjoyable date idea in mind and can toss it into the conversation.

Some people have a tough time scheduling dates also far out in breakthrough. Involve the man in the date organizing. Be sure to ask for his input, but just make sure that by the end of your discussion that you have a date on your schedule that you are confident will work out.

3. Use your words wisely. The scheduling of your date is not likely to be done in person. Instead, the communication these days happens typically using voice and message. This means that the only things connecting you and the guy are the words you choose to speak. Be flirty, but the company. Remind him how interested he is in you. Enamor him with a spray of light discussion before entering the details of scheduling. The teasing part should not be too harsh, but it's essential to be strong in the facet of organizing, so it doesn't get involved in an extended arrangement. Review your alternatives of possible things to do and when to do them, and then reach a verdict. A final thought about the future date is necessary to it occurring. Keep in mind, do not let the discussion end before reiterating the date info (day of the week, time, place). If he doesn't move your communication onward, after that, you may want to consider it a red (or at least) a yellow flag.

You need to have at least one phone call before your date. Whether the phone call is partially to arrange the date or it comes after the first organizing, always try to conclude your discussion with the date info for clarity.

Try to keep texting on the playful side of the spectrum by having light and easygoing conversations. Or text possibly some hrs before you are scheduled to meet simply to validate you are on your way/on time (something teasing like "life is excellent from my end, and I'm on time- see u soon." That way, if any type of problem comes up at the last min, there is a way of open communication to deal with them.

Get Him to Chase You - Play Hard to Get Like a Pro

Do you want to get him to chase you? It delights men and gets them interested. Men want to work for the women in their lives, and by playing hard to get, you can make it possible for him to do just that.

Difficult to get, yet possible.

The first thing you need to do is to make sure you have a proper meaning of hard to get. Because you have made it feel impossible for him to capture you, you don't want to get him to chase you and then have him give up. To make this occur, you will wish to see to it that you balance everything out. The secret to an excellent game of hard to get is balance.

-Capture his focus.

You can not get him to chase you if you do not have his interest beforehand. After that, look your ideal by stressing your most exceptional attributes and understating your worst features, making use of garments, makeup, and devices. You end this with some teasing, and you will record his attention for sure.

Follow the regulations.

The regulations of tough to get are comfortable, yet they need to be well stabilized to make it work. You need to be mindful to follow them, but if it indeed works better, a slightly different way to make it more balanced for your connection, it will certainly be alright to readjust and also tweak them.

1. Let him make the very first move.

2. When you go out, make sure he has a great deal of enjoyment and that you have a lot of fun.

3. Do not call him or seek him out. Allow him to do the job.

4. Be active in your life, and do not wait on his phone call.

5. See to it; you allowed him to know how much fun you had, which you are eagerly anticipating his following phone call or

your next date. This will certainly balance out the truth that you aren't actively seeking him. You want him to understand you are interested.

6. Have times when you are hectic and miss his call or place a date off. To do this right, you want to ensure you call him back or attempt to reschedule. You may be busy Friday evening and deal to go out on Saturday evening or meet for Sunday brunch.

It is all about balance. You intend to get him to chase you and keep chasing you until he has captured you. This will take some job and some care, but it well worth it in the end.

CHAPTER THREE

Flirt your Way through his Heart

So you have a crush on your officemate, but he doesn't seem to understand. You wish to win his heart, but you simply do not knowhow. You've discovered the art of teasing, but you do not know how to start.

How can you play the game of invitation if you're not sure how to do it?

When will winning be satisfying?

What does being a terrific seductress means?

The legislation of temptation and flirting does not call for a shapely body form or an excellent size; what it requires is a set of unique strategies that you can use despite your age and your job. Below is the power that you need to exhibit if you want to keep the fire burning.

=Proper Preparation.

The right means to start how to flirt with men is to head to your restroom. Pick a lovely elegance soap and have a good bath. Pick the hot dress that you can use without damaging your firm outfit code. For the final touches, apply light makeup to make you look charming and young and spray on some fragrance. Appropriate preparation work starts before you leave your room.

=Let Your Eyes Make the First Move.

He is starting teasing from a range. How is this feasible? Well, let your eyes do the talking. His table could be in the room, but your eyes can go near him. Send him "the appearance." Lingering eye get in touch with changes every little thing. Continue gazing up until he observes you and makes sure that he will notice you taking a look at him. When he does, send him a guilty look without regretting. This act is sexy and attractive.

=Time to Talk

So your sticking around eye call didn't convince him to find over, did it? This means it's time for you to go through his means and talk. Men love to see this kind of self-confidence from women, and also this is the right time to flirt with men. Before you part your lips and start saying "hi," think of the perfect topic that men wish to chat regarding. If you do not understand anything about his likes, simply let him talk concerning himself - "him" is among men's preferred subjects.

=Be the Operator.

Make sure that points are smooth-going, or this guy will think that you're doing the same with other men. Another resourceful "just how to flirt with men" pointer is to make him believe he's seducing you. Men despise it when they know that women are attempting to attract them. So let him assume that he's doing just that and make him fall for you - hitting two birds with one rock!

=Praise, Compliment, Compliment!

Compliment him to flirt with him efficiently. Praise him for winning his heart. Compliment him to make him feel unique. There are only many things that you can do by merely making him think that you appreciate him and his jobs. You can compliment him on anything but never overdo it. There is simply truly something with "praise" that men love the woman that does it much better.

As women, all of us know that men just chat a different language. This language barrier works in two ways. We listen to things in different ways, and we say things differently.

Being increased with brother and working in a male-dominated market for 20 years taught me the real worth of getting male/female interaction. Now, as a mom of girl/boy doubles, I can see the same things happening; it is a sex issue. To understand a guy and to get the most effective out of him, following his language is essential.

Let's consider three areas where miscommunication can take place:

1. The first is WHY we are speaking.

If you are flirting because you intend to look for a deep, meaningful, personal link with a male you've just met, and also he's flirting because he's usually a teasing, flirtatious person or has been shown teasing is merely part of the process, you are automatically in a setting where one or both of you is bound to experience some embarrassment or pain. You would appropriately feel most of the complication and even rage if you understood he was just "tinkering you" when you on your own seemed like you were starting up the first steps of courtship.

2. The second place that develops miscommunication is HOW we talk.

This is where "tone" becomes so vital. Typically, increasing your voice somewhat at the end of a sentence is understood to work as an inquiry. At the same time, a level tone is usually understood to be a declaration, and dropping at the end is a command.

A typical example: "You look charming tonight." The man that says such a thing is often speaking at face value. He merely means you look charming tonight. You may hear you look beautiful tonight, which could indicate that you do not look attractive at the time the man has seen or sees you. You might, after that begin to question what's wrong with your look and why he feels the demand to criticize it.

On the other hand, your analysis might also be legitimate. He could have placed just the right articulation on the word to give it that meaning, transforming the praise into a well-positioned barb but because words, "You look charming tonight," audio nothing yet free of charge, he has to go. He can save face.

These types of interactions are typical in women circles, where there's a very subtle war for social status that occurs amongst all but the closest of good friends. Praises that are anything but, with all capacity to retaliate gotten rid of, are a typical usage of women language.

3. The third-place where speech is likely to fail is where it insists, or indicates, power and control speech, which shows up or give commands against a statement which supplies criticism or appears to provide objection is just one of the stickiest and most challenging kinds of speech to handle.

Usually, within a connection, both parties must be able to express their needs, but the power dynamic is the area where things are most unsafe. The power dynamic is what's most greatly up in arms between men and women, and where things start to get a bit unmanageable.

No place is this more apparent than in the principle of 'direct' speech vs. 'indirect' speech.

Directness in the language is connected with direct statements and commands that are not softened or implied, such as 'quit stating that' or 'close that door.'.

Indirectness involves softening or indicating significances as opposed to mentioning them straight, such as, 'I would certainly choose it if you would not claim things like that' or 'I am cool.'.

Men, who usually react to and use straight language, take a sentence spoken in indirect, women, word like 'I 'd favor it if you would not state things like that' at face worth. In their mind, they now understand what you do not, such as. Unless they have figured out female talk, the indicated message - saying things like that'- will merely not register.

Remember, you are trying to find MISTER Right, in which Misters make things in a different way than Missuses. Knowing that men communicate in different ways from women, not much better, not even worse, only different, is getting the connection right.

How To Read A Mans Body Language

Knowing how to read a guy's body language can give a girl more insight into what he's feeling and thinking than what he speaks. Understanding the body language of the male, you are wanting to meet or are now in connection with can give you some incredible understandings of what he is thinking and feeling and also help you in knowing what you need to do to make the connection to the next level.

One of the other visible body language signs to seek in a man is where his eyes are going. While he doesn't need to be looking deep into your eyes for minutes at a time, if a guy doesn't explore your eyes, sometimes there's a probability he's not all that curious about you. The one caveat with this piece of ideals is reluctant people who could be right into you but unable to explore your eyes. You ought to be able to tell how shy a guy is by clues such as if you approached him first or if when he grins, his lips are pressed firmly together. He's pleased to see you but terrified to open his mouth and say something. A lot of people with at least fundamental social skills must have the ability to look into women's eyes sometimes.

Another part of a man's body to be aware of is his hands. Men that motion a whole lot with their hands while speaking to a woman are attempting to hold her interest. While not all men will connect this way, the majority of them will.

If a guy moves toward you or leans your means while speaking to you, he is possibly interested in getting to know you much better. Men, for the most part, do not like to be explicitly crowded when they are dealing with one person, so if he turns in your direction, he's probably prepared to take it to the next level.

When the women show up cold can imply much more, what lots of women consider typical politeness such as opening a door for them or giving up their layer. When a guy cares for something, he desires to take care of it and protect it. This goes for the women in his life. He will go out of his means to make sure she is protected and comfortable. If a guy is treating you this way, consider it an excellent sign. If he doesn't practice these little acts of kindness, it's a hint for the women to dive deeper right into what is happening in the relationship.

Knowing how to review a male's body language can give a lady a remarkable benefit when it comes to an understanding of him, what he's thinking, and, most notably, how he feels about you. Once you recognize this, you can, after that, began to use this understanding to attract him closer to you.

How to Identify Flirting Body Language

Kinesics is the research study of body language and its significances known as a direct response from the limbic system in the brain; body language is a subconscious action many people can't manage. Just viewers will observe other people's body language, but they do not see their own. In the olden day's body language is used as a useful tool for survival and breeding. This is still true today, as body language is a specific response in the direction of how we feel and how we think others think regarding us.

Women who are attracting the attention of men will subconsciously send flirting body language as a signal for him to approach her. Some women use flirting with encouraging men to contact them so that they can slowly pick a suitable companion.

A female that is all ready for sex will sometimes like to allow the male to make amove. If a man is brought into a woman and needs her in bed, sexual body motions sent by slow brushing of rounded damp objects such as the top of the glass will certainly tease and promote him. Women's body language can be tempting and exceptionally strong to men.

Body language has been relied on kind of interaction considering that time immemorial. Before the growth of communications, everybody interacts using body language to signify what they want and what they are presumptuous. Depressing to say, as humans grow, their ability to read body language began to decline because humans tend to concentrate too much attention on verbal communication. Some people are incredibly good at reading body signals and controlling them to their advantage. For some unknown factors, some men are brought in like a magnet by women's body language also when on regular occasions, they do not know what women are saying. Talking too much makes the world spin for men. That's why the idiom "Action speaks louder than word" exists.

Mothers and kids began their first communication with body signals as well. Infants particularly can see and know the stress or happiness or temper on people's faces and emotions. That is just how they establish that likes them or not. People that claimed babies don't want them are people that do not know, such as infants. Body signal is difficult to hide and is probably one of the most accurate and honest signals on exactly how we feel. Minxes are women that can act out false body gesture to use their sexual allure to make use of men indirectly.

CHAPTER FOUR

Why Men Love Hos

The first thing that crosses a man's mind when he meets a new female is how she looks. When a man meets a modern woman, he automatically judges her level of pretty. It doesn't matter how phony any of it is; men do not care where it came from as long as it looks excellent inactivity!

To get a male and flirt with him in a method where you stroke, his vanity will always win him over. Praises, flirty sass, as well as sex-related body language, will bring a male to his knees. Men don't know for sure that you're drawn into them; they presume it.

A woman that does not look half as good as Mila can stroll up to a guy, make eye contact, praise his smile, and give off crazy body language, and magic occurs. This guy's brain transforms her from a seven to a nine because she's kind, showing a rate of interest, and filling up that insecure hole that all men have. That's called beauty.

The strippers that make one of the most cash aren't necessarily the prettiest; they're the ones with the most active discussion, the ones that place a male secure, which makes him feel good-looking. They appeal the cash out of his wallet for longer than that one track he promised he wasn't going to pass by. There are corny strippers who are more than happy to take their clothes off and ask people if they want a dance, yet they're lap-dancing like their shadow boxing, numb to the fact and dry as hell in their salesmanship. Allow a stripper that comes by with something fascinating to claim that she's a human being and not just making the rounds, and she's going to compel that man to beg the ATM. Her bare breast and butt socializing didn't draw him; her appeal pulled him by making use of a male's need to feel unique in a room complete of rival males. That's Ho charm, these women who not only come off as sexy but who likewise recognize how to make a guy feel like he's the center of deep space.

Charm alone won't astound a guy to the point where he's treating you to Vegas trips just because know what men look for in a lady physically and what different other women look for competitively. Many of the high-quality men will be turned off because they do not want to be seen strolling down the road or cuffing a girl that dresses like that.

As a woman wanting to win in any type of area, you need to resolve your allure in manner ins, which leads to you being embraced first, and after that, you can unload the vast weapons. Dressing provocatively will get you to hit on, yet it's only because people believe you're secure. Leave something to the creativity, not as many, yet enough where you will certainly at least garner some respect. Hos invest a great deal of time perfecting their look because they know other women will try to classify them in a range of men who will positively after that be affected by that, "Your dick might diminish if you place it in that," slander. Gown not sleazy yet attractive, since your hustle will not work if a man sees you, and your top, initially look.

No matter if you're skinny or fat, small breast with large hips, big tits with no ass, and every little thing between-- know your body and know what looks excellent on you. I'm not talking about looking in the mirror and assuming that it matches, go more in-depth and focus on your clothes as if you were choosing out a Halloween outfit. If you're going to the store to get some hairspray, use your sweatpants but make sure they fit the proper way which you seem like a goddess in them, not a bloated girl on her period that simply discovered something to toss on.

Every single time you tip out of your home is a possibility to bring in somebody who might change your life, so always look beautiful. A thirsty guy will talk with any type of woman; they're just playing the parts. A pussy hunter will speak with any woman showing skin because men comprehend that women's sex trap for a reason-- they want sex. Sponsors and tricks aren't competing after pussy; they're looking for signs that you're various, that you're top quality and not someone that the world has tasted. If you expect a guy to treat you like a princess, you can't run around looking like a destitute neither can you walk around looking desperate like you tipped out of the brothel. It's an equilibrium of makeup, hairdo, and fashion, and the only way to know that you've obtained it ideal is to be your examination-- Do I look sexy as fuck today in my messy bun, broken pants, and lip gloss? Yes, I do! Reach that level psychologically, and your allure can't be touched.

Men assume they understand everything regarding women because, in all sincerity, a lot of women do behave equally. The majority of men are biased because they have seen how women from different backgrounds all do the same precise things as well as respond in the same specific ways. What separates Hos from this regular passive-aggressive, connection lusting selection of females is that they don't give a fuck.

Ho Appeal

Because these girls are all girls keeping it light and fun, a Ho's perspective is the sexiest thing about her.

Hos do not ask a question about love or partnerships; they stay in the current. Hos does not return a phone call to speak about that missed; they call to talk shit. Hos, don't worry about other girls. This habit is one-of-a-kind; it perplexes a male to the point where he's genuinely surprised. To spend an evening with a girl who doesn't mind describing him as sexy, who knows how to clothe in a way that turns him on without awkward him, and who genuinely couldn't care less about being his sweetheart, is an enjoyable and zero-pressure scenario. It tells a guy that she wants that prick, yet she's not trying to imprison that penis. That she's weird, but she's not a fanatic that every guy has probably been within. Most significantly, it says that she's incredible enough to drop his guard around without the worry of angering her with his talk about the good looks of other women or otherwise being prepared for a relationship.

A man's biggest fear is dedication, while a female's most significant anxiety is not discovering

As a female, you can rest and say you're satisfied being single and don't need a guy. Still, you will likely slip up and reveal things that give you away because, most of the time, saying you're single and happy is a defense device to avoid being harmed once again. Because of this uniqueness, men want to maintain these women on the team permanently and will certainly go above and beyond to make it happen.

Since their fantastic perspective integrated with their appeal and sex appeal is Disneyland for guys, hos win. It's a dream world where a guy can kick back with a girl who doesn't push him appealing.

If you give any man a choice of going to school and having to put in a real job or going to an enjoyment park where he doesn't have to do crap but pay the expense of admission and get a few presents, he's going to pick the fun expensive alternative because it's risk-free, comfortable, and tension free. They aren't simple sexually, but they are straightforward emotionally, and also that's the puzzle that the majority of women can not fix. The typical women's mind can not comprehend just how terrifying the idea of commitment is to men that desire to have a good time.

How to Online Date the Ho Way

If your ass is what obtains you the most interest, best that side sight shot, so the world recognizes what you're working with. As soon as you have your photo, go authorize up for a paid dating website, not a freebie, because those are rest paradises for broke men that enjoy homing window stores as if they can afford you. Now, it's time to locate a rich man.

You can rest on the web and find all kinds of "gold digger" dating sites where men look for what they call "sugar children" to ruin. While I don't question that some of these men are enrollers, they are most likely the most horrible of the bunch that is using these websites as a choice to companion solutions. This isn't Escort Education; this is Ho Tactics, and once again, I must aim out that the point is to get what you want without giving your body.

Let me present the most significant Ho thirst catch innovation because of the marvel bra-- social networking. Facebook is a world where you can connect with new baes and old boos and see where they work, where they live and research almost every element of their lives if you can get a good friend demand approved. Twitter gives you 140 personalities to reveal off aspects of your wit and post images.

How many of you use it to make money, gain condition, or attach with a man that will fly you anywhere you want to go? The majority of women on social networking sites are much more worried about showing up rival women by getting likes, gaining fans, or having their opinions agreed upon by arbitrary broke niggas that are someplace jerking off in their mom's basement. Smart Hos aren't concerned with how many handsome young boys retweet them or how many fake-gay ladies designate them their Woman Crush Wednesday for fond memories or tell K. Michelle how they can not wait to see her jointly. Smart Hos know how to use every one of these websites in a certain way to advertise themselves.

When I say advertise, I'm not speaking about some ratchet booking e-mail to verify your model or host parties, nor am I describing a link to some jewelry collection or T-shirt internet site that you run. Hos promote themselves! If you're nicely built, your body is your resume. If you have the face of a siren, that mug is your crawler internet. Your words become the quicksand that will catch your method if you're aggressive and amusing. No matter what classification you are, know where you are the strongest. I do not want to listen to, "I'm fast witted and a dime," I question that because if that is true, you would be out in the roads turning the Ho Tactics right into a condo.

I once saw somebody ask a valet if he can sit in the traveler side of a person's Maserati and take a picture. I visualize that flick ended up on "the gram" and got him to a man like me who is seeing this transpire, that guy is a clown, yet to the rest of the world, he's a Hollywood baller. That man doesn't have to pull up in that car and truck; he can say it is in the store after getting rammed after the club, take her back to the hotel, and make her think she's around to lay beside a male that can change her life.

That's how frauds make use of dumb Hos and naïve women.

The second rule of thumb is to aim for men on the level you can manage. Some of you may be adorable enough for Drake to follow you, yet Drake's not going to allow you to enter his pockets the same way he would let Bria from Hooters [16] come to his pockets. To these heavyweight celebrities, you are one of several internet THOTS [17]. Unless you're in their city for the weekend and eager to come to get gambled at the Four Seasons, they mostly will not entertain you the same ways they would delight a person with status like R&B starlet Christina Milian or perhaps a girl they met in public. Know what level you're and also pursue men who aren't always in the spotlight. Those are the non-celebrity kinds that may have enough money to damage your pricey itches. If you only concentrate on the Dallas Cowboy or Persian Prince, then you're going to get lost in the Ho shuffle and lose out.

Know what men on the net reply to-- look firstly, personality second.

Your character. To get his focus, you follow up with style. Some ladies simply retweet in hopes that they will get a guy's attention or as an image in hopes he will be satisfied adequate to follow back.

Note that men with cash or power are not monitoring every online interaction in the same means bored bottoms do, so you have to be aggressive to get a male's attention. The reason is, you need to be prepared to go for a guy if you believe he's a gold ticket, don't think that since you're pretty in your account picture that every male will feel the same.

No example

Maria is also active, Hoping up real to play on the web, yet she places her reluctant best friend into the Imani is what we can refer to as cute, not always a bombshell, yet slightly enough to get attention when she feels like dressing up. The problem is Imani isn't outbound in public; she's soft-spoken and scheduled, and usually gets lost in the shuffle when she's around alpha females like Maria. Imani sees the life that Maria is living in. Also, while she's not after a full-on enroller, she can use the money for moving and perhaps get her bills paid until she graduates from university.

For the first time in her life, Imani takes to her social networking account with a money goal. As I said earlier, you should know what you want from these men first and after that placed in the job to get that without resolving for disturbances like sex or a sweetheart. To blow in the wind with no clear Ho intent, will net you bullshit results. Imani's goal is to find a man that can give adequate cash for her to vacate by January 1st. It's currently October, to make sure that puts stress on her to act now as opposed to putting it off like some indecisive Basica. Imani starts by buying her online look. She's going to develop new avatars for Facebook, Instagram, and Twitter accurately that show various aspects of her individuality. Lighting, makeup, and hair are one of the essential devices at this phase of the game. Hair can be difficult, despite if you have long moving blonde hair, natural swirls, or are weaved up; you have to go with the look that you like the many. My choice has always been toward longer hair, so I'm going to use this as my example, but I am not the male standard. Whatever hairdo makes you feel great is what you go to the hairdresser to make.

The last action is proper space lighting; you have to make sure you radiance, be it in a picture or a selfie made to look as if it were taking in the moment, aka the "caught me sliding" staged photo. I mean face shots for Instagram and Twitter, and conserve the full body for Facebook. If you aren't comfortable with a complete collection, after that face shots with all 3, it's not made or damage.

Since Imani has made use of the choice ability of Anna Wintour to handpick the most effective pictures for her different profiles, she has to filter out the waters with a blatant thirst trap. With her face light on make-up, but still, blemish-free, she publishes a picture looking upset. As opposed to choosing the passé

#NoFilter tag, she blasts out, "Just awakened, #Badhair day," or if it's a nighttime shot, "Just got out of course resembling #TheStruggle." These are staged pictures, yet they catch Imani in the moment minus a smile, which in turn will make the males on social media want to kiss her butt by guaranteeing her that she's still a poor bitch. This isn't about thirst trapping undesirables; it's regarding evaluating your brand-new default keep an eye out. Remember, this is still the way you look in your avatar, minus a little makeup, so this is going to be your brand moving forward. Regardless of if it's you smarten upped or semi-natural, it has to promote you like a dollar.

Going back to #TheStruggle thirst catch photo, Imani will understand how effective her brand-new appearance is by the action from the public. Imani has about 1700 Instagram followers, which means she possibly gets 30-60 sort while the stalkers prowl waiting for a reason to show themselves. This attention doesn't gas Imani, she's not below for the affection of unfamiliar people, or to hear what loser wants to spouse her up.

What kind of men are obtaining cash but still have time to be regularly on the web? Pro athletes! Unlike CEO's who are more likely working 16-hour days or artists that do more promoting than thirsting, athletes have a great deal of downtime between periods. Also, because their jobs need constant ESPN updates, they typically have their phones in hand. Imani does not know much about sporting activities; she joys for the teams with the brightest shades and hashtags #TeamLakers off the toughness that she as soon as brought a Kobe Bryant jacket gown in secondary school. Where does a woman

It's October, and also the World Series is going on, which implies that all yet 2 Major League Baseball teams are at residence enjoying. Imani would preferably want

a tall Basketball player. Still, that period is merely beginning, and she's not likely to obtain the full attention of a gamer that's on the road every few days being chased by resort groupies. Baseball is, so she Twitter searches for a couple of baseball tags, and seeks that confirmed indication.

It takes a couple of hrs, but Imani finds a potential mark whose twitter active. He's eye-catching enough and plays for the Pittsburg Pirates. Imani lives down south, yet that doesn't hinder her because being long distance with an off-season professional athlete shouldn't be an element if he's making "I'll fly out" cash. Although this guy isn't a home name or among the highly pertained to gamers, he works paying more than the fools in her city, so why not go for it.

Imani doesn't add the mark right away; a blind follow will be ignored. Imani instead piggybacks on his point to make another critic show that she's on the same wavelength as him. Imani knows that being pretty enough to get a response usually means pretty sufficient to follow, and she guesses.

Imani is out Instagram to go with this guy as well as she's not on Twitter to be his subtweet boo. Shy women defeat around the shrub; Hos go to the source of the cash as soon as they are given the environment-friendly light. Imani takes the discussion personally within 24 hrs of the following. She has straight access to this guy, which means she can let loose the full power of her personality in a way that she could not do in person. Imani doesn't hurry to give her telephone number or ask for his. To meet with a guy and after that, jump in his DM requesting the numbers stinks of jumpoff. She isn't a baseball fan and also needs to passion in Googling random spunk to discuss. Instead, she scours his timeline and takes not a subject she can work on. In this situation, it's an argument concerning J Cole versus Wale. She DMs him in support of J Cole and begins to lure him with a musical conversation. For the following two days, Imani will proceed to bring up arbitrary discussion points to build a relationship with him. On the other hand, her Instagram twit pics get sexier and sexier, knowing that this man's thirst is what she's trying to catch.

It's been less than a week, and this Major League mark asks Imani for her number, she teases him a bit, because to just give it out could repaint her as very cheap. Imani lays the policies down in a playful method, "I only give my number to men that use it, not rest on it." Of course, the mark says that he will use it. To hook him harder, she gives it out with the cautiousness of,

"Let's see how soon you keep your word." Ho Tactic 101, Imani has tested this male's vanity, and it won't be even more than 20 minutes before he calls to accept that difficulty.

When Imani has him on the phone one on one, standard Ho Tactics apply. Study his life and see how generous he has the prospective to be. Since he's several miles away, Imani can't do the date test, yet she can do a "mail me something" test.

CHAPTER FIVE

How to Flirt Hos Way

Women have become so bad at flirting that men can not inform if the average chick is being friendly or if she is genuinely interested. This leaves a big opening for women that knows the ins and outs of flirting with controlling the game on every level. When I spoke to a girl, who was irritated with her lack of ability to get this guy at her child's school to ask her out, they would say "hi" and talk about the weather. She assumed that he did not like her, so she acted sheepishly instead of pursuing him. I asked if he spoke first or if she spoke? She said he would take-off most times when he even chased her down outside to asked about her Christmas because he hadn't seen her in a few weeks. I then asked what she had done to show him that she liked him. Crickets. Her feedback was, "What am I meant to do, enter his arms?".

Again, women see in extremes, instead of accepting that a lot of points in life need you to read between the lines while using tact. It doesn't matter if you're speaking concerning the weather condition or your boring weekend, a lady that understands the power of voice inflection, romantic eye contact, and doesn't mind blinking a sly smile can make those subjects sexier than discussing his favorite bedroom setting.

Hos win out over a lot of women because they aren't worried about selling themselves. What eye-catching, well-read, yet timid women stop working to realize that no matter how good you are, you do not come with a billboard listing these characteristics. You do not have a supporter running behind you like, "Sara owns a business, doesn't.

Who else is there to educate a top-shelf male that you are a top-shelf woman? Some men will do this, and it still does not fix the problem because an introverted woman who is afraid to climb to the occasion won't know how to communicate with this guy in a way that's engaging and playful. A regular enlightened yet awkward female will certainly stumble through discussion, over laugh, have pockets of stressful silence, and also leave the guy thinking she's odd.

Let's support a bit and keep it real. Most men with money, status, or those things that will make him a perfect trick or sponsor, aren't going to walk up on 90% of the women in his city. Not because they aren't pretty, but because they may not be worth the risk in his eyes. Every man has his taste when it comes to attraction, and just because he thinks you are cute doesn't mean he's willing to put his feelings on the line by approaching you. I've had at least two girlfriends that I would have never approached in public. If it weren't for being a friend of a friend, I would have never gotten to know them enough to want to be with them because they didn't fit that flawless category I pretended to need when I initially laid eyes on them. If you know the mind of man, then you understand looks change after a conversation, a connection, or flirting. That charm I spoke of earlier will win over that picky man who rated you a six from across the room.

To stroll over and compliment him, make him grin, share a story, etc. You go from "she aight," to "she sexy," and you did not also reapply any type of lipstick. This is what gives them the confidence to walk up to any man, no matter how she looks, because the discussion will always update the look!

Tricks may still approach you, yet that's not the point. I need you to agree that finding the right man to hustle will generally require you to make the first move. There are women that men think about "the following level" beautiful, and they will approach them in public if the setting is right. Indeed, Mr. Heir to a coffee firm can chase you down if you're what he's looking for that night, but why leave it up to his discernment. Why let this trick choose you when you can select him and from the move have him assuming you're fixated? A guy of methods has a million excuses not to pursue a lady, but the main thing at work is that the male ego doesn't want to be curved. To spark the conversation starts the process because guys get overeager with thoughts of, "She spoke first, that must mean she wants to fuck." Let him wag his tail; you're going to lead that dog by the leash and drain his pockets way before you drain his nut sack. Do not fear conversation! Know that for this to work, you have to check your ego at the door. You can't operate under the rules of, wait for a sign or lure a man in with eye contact. Given that these men won't risk asking you out of pride, you have to do what Hos do, go to that mine to dig for gold.

How to Communicate with Men

The character of guys is stiffer compared to females, and this should be understood throughout discussions. Use specific numbers when talking to men. By using a more rational style highlighting numbers and figures, men will be able to comprehend much better.

What Should You Do to Switch your Man's Clock?

There's a secure way to switch off your man's dating clock: merely never let a single pattern or stereotype be revealed in what you say, how you say it, how you dress, or what you demonstratively anticipate from the man—consistent spontaneity. Keep him guessing. Outsmart him. Use everything I've told you in this book to shatter his hourglass into a million pieces. You can do it. He'll be sitting there looking at you, silently identifying your end date, when suddenly you'll toss him for a ring. You'll say something or do something that triggers cognitive dissonance. You could blurt out, "I've always asked why men are into seeing two women together" or "I never get wild until I'm with someone for a while." Saying things like this plays right into his "desire list." Such comments are specific enough to get him thinking, but not so concrete that they symbolize that you'll deliver. Now he has to go back to square one. It's not a game; it's just smart.

I love it when a woman surprises men. I also love it when I believe a woman is simple, and it turns out that she's using the men. These are the women who get the best men, and every single one of you has the prospective to be that woman.

The Problem and the Fix with Flirty Outing.

Here's the problem: Any man worth his salt is going to pick a place where the two of you can get to know each other, which will most likely be either a bar or restaurant. The good news is that it's right to make suggestions on the mood and tempo surrounding the outing. If he's hell-bent on a particular place, then go online and check it out or ask for the excellent date restaurant in the city.

Pick bars or restaurants where the vibe is relaxed. Avoid pricey or excessively fashionable hotspots. You're going for a place with great food, excellent service, reasonable prices, low-level noise, and people like you two.

In the Suburbs.

Try to go to a place where you both know but rarely frequent-- Remember that depending on your choice, the whole town may know about your date. Or pick a place you've both only heard of but would like to try together. This could become "your place" if things work out.

How to Flirt with Guys without Risky Rejection or Embarrassment

Flirting is among those points that seem to be a force of habit to some, but is a whole international language to others. Like with kissing, if you also get to know about it, it just comes to be more robust.

Try to remember that flirting is meant to be fun. Don't take it seriously. If you give it too much weight, it comes to be downright scary-- so loosen up. (I know, easier said than done.).

A lively, flirty small talk is like a tennis match. It can feel electrifying when you get into a good groove with somebody. Some moderate flirting can be the press he needs to make his move if you're interested in a guy that is a little worried.

-Component 1: Flirting Face to Face.

Praise him and flirt him.

You may not know it, yet men like praises and compliments aren't as openly given to men as they are to women. Men don't have a group of cheerleaders telling them how impressive they look before heading out for a night.

Search him for something special to compliment. Try to avoid common remarks such as, "I like your t-shirt." Go the extra mile. For instance: "Wow, that t-shirt brings out the environment-friendly in your eyes.".

If you mumble it or look somewhere else while you're speaking or overdo it, it's simply not going to have the same effect. Relax your nerves and look him straight in the eye when you talk.

Do not go for anything that he can be delicate around. If he has big muscle mass, you can make a joke about him being scrawny if he's scrawny, most definitely do not mention it even as a joke!

Your purpose right here is to be seen as naughty, not as one of the guys.

-Smile.

For one reason or another, many women think that being an ice queen that plays hard to get is an acceptable method of dating. Overlook it instantly if you've been given that advice. A kind, the happy lady is always more eye-catching than a sullen one.

Chuckling, grinning, and being generally bright are all extremely eye-catching. Pay attention and react warmly when he tells a story.

CHAPTER SIX

Seduction Talking Point

What is seduction?

* Seduction is the art of using sex-related attraction to get a goal.

* The objective is not always sex-related intimacy. For instance, tv commercials unappealing young versions for advertising a hot and hip image for their solutions and also items. The sexy part motivates you to buy their items.

* Then again, there is hooking or cruising up, in which the seducer's goal is consummated in a one-night stand.

* More generally, the objective is of seduction is to win over true love. Below, physical attraction is type in making that critical impression. Past that, a long-lasting relationship can just come around by common interests and individual chemistry.

* The least typical type of temptation includes reconnaissance. Below, bribery and blackmail are the most common approaches to getting intelligence information, which is the ultimate goal. But seduction for industrial-as opposed to state-sponsored-

espionage has had a long and healthy run in this country until the Economic Espionage Act of 1996 was passed into law.

How does one seduce?

* To be seductive, one first has to look sexy. Look counts for that first perception, and you want to make your intended dream date think, "Wow!" before you even open your mouth.

* For the majority of young people, the key to a good look is exercise, diet regimen, correct pet grooming, and a wardrobe that matches your environment. Most times, this prevails sense. That ribbed sweater, which hugs your trim figure, looks explicitly good at a ski resort, but you might think twice about taking it on an exotic cruise. For men, pants and a flannel t-shirt are perfect for a hiking trip, yet are not the best for anywhere, where the girls spruce up. If the gals go with all that problem to look good, you need to show some effort also.

* Let's say you have all the classic attributes of homeliness. You have jowly cheeks, baggy eyes, a declining chin, a connected nose, and thick eyebrows. Let'salsoassume that you're disciplined. Your weight is under control, and you graduated as the best student in your class in college. How do you make

quality? As a last hope, take into consideration plastic surgical treatment.

* If you've paid approximately $100-to-$ 200 thousand bucks to finish your higher education and learning, would not it behoove you to spend possibly $20 thousand for therapy by a first-rate cosmetic surgeon? This might appear extreme, yet psychology research studies have always shown that attractive people are more successful in the company and gain more money. You could find this superficial, but it's a reality, and it gives you a rock-solid rationalization past accessible vanity to go under the blade.

How does one start a conversation?

* If you're an appealing woman, it's simple. Men will usually flirt with you. Of program that cute guy, whom you're dying to meet, has a severe case of shyness. Think like a spy. Phase a small catastrophe like unintentionally running across him and dropping your belongings. This allows him to be a knight in shining armor. When he helps you take your stuff (and he will), make your step.

How far do you intend to be? That's up to you. Be warm and free. Now, if you've done your study, you know that he is a rabid Yankees fan. Do you assume he could be curious about those two tickets you have for the game against the Red Sox?

* When it comes to drawing the opposite sex, men in-group are not as focused as women. I could say that most men are downright lazy. Around them, women are producing warning signals, and the men are just clueless. Consider all the high maintenance a lady in waiting has gone through with her hair, her makeup, her color combination, and her jewelry. It all begs to be noticed and commented on. What does her mirror tell her? She talks to it every day.

Keys to Seduction of the Opposite Sex

According to some psychological research studies, women who read enchanting novels make love to their partners 74% times even more than those women that do not. We have not come across this before!

Before Reality TV and the vast porn sector in print and on the web, sex was indeed an enigma. Even more than that, women were hard to get. Naturally, you can obtain the service ladies, yet if wished to obtain a girl of your dreams, then it was challenging. With morals as well as traditional culture, it simply was not possible. Naturally, there are now many more places like clubs, workplaces, environments, and also bars where you can meet sensible along with good looking women with a high level of knowledge. No matter what sort of woman you meet, deep down, they all desire to be loved.

Temptation isn't a two-minute skip in the bed and goes off to sleep ritual. If it is mechanical, then the women will not remain with you. They would just pack their bags and also provide you a cold shoulder. What you require to do is to make the temptation procedure erotic. Exactly how should you take treatment if this trouble?

-Stand up to The Urge To Rush Into Things

What you require to recognize is that if you hurry right into the act of seduction, it reveals that you aren't sure concerning yourself. You are frightened of falling short or of committing. You require to delicately approach her, take her in your arms, as well as erotically take off her garments.

-Have An Air Of Mystery

She probably knows how it will end up, but how will you set about completion? There needs to be a mystery aspect regarding the entire procedure. Do not disclose yourself. Take off the secret layer one by one. Take off the shadow and also let her to the exploration. When she gradually starts to uncover your body, respond similarly. Every lady has a soft area. Touch the part, and also it can send a wave of eroticism over her. Ask her where she would love to be touched, and in response, she would do the very same to you. The end is as essential as the means to get to the end.

-Ask Her About Her Sexual Fantasies

All women have sex-related fantasies. The giant adventure of doing something can obtain a female to be exceptionally sensual. There are several sex-related dreams that a lady has.

How to Seduce the Ho Way

Ladies are meeting men extremely because the purpose is to ensure he's credible and truthful enough to be a partner or potential hubby. Hos substitute the interview procedure with the seducing phase because they know the way to a guy's budget starts with his penis. Since you're not looking to bond on a real level, his life store and previous relationships don't matter when you're trying to hustle a man. All a Ho needs to know is if he's paid, how paid, and how generous he wants to be with that money. When you establish that you have a guy that is eager to treat you to excellent ways, you dig the hooks is much more in-depth by using what a guy wants most against him- sex. Ho'srole is to be a fantasy female. A lady that pays attention isn't judgmental, never emphasizes time or interest, and, most importantly, knows how to be a dirty whore. I advise you that these are the non-sex methods, so if the way you've been shown to seduce is by letting him stick the suggestion in, you're going to toss that tactical plan out to be a master of making a guy orgasm, without using your pussy.

Attracting is the development of teasing, yet girls who are great flirts commonly freeze when it's time to get down and filthy.

To make a guy see you as hot, desirable, and essential, you need to show him that you are a great time. What makes you amusing? What makes you edgy? What makes you unpleasant? What makes you different? That's not rhetorical; a response that in your head right now. After you've come up with those responses, look back on the last time you were on a first date and consider how you highlighted those four things in such a way that a guy could co-sign your responses. Most of you can't respond to the question or aren't sure, yet the reality is in the outcomes. Because a shot of your personality is weaker than a Peter Gunz late-night alibi, you didn't separate yourself.

The last first date I went on was with an incredibly corny woman. Here's what made her trite: during that dinner, she didn't say anything intriguing. She just poked fun at my jokes and played timid when I made a perverted remark. In the movie theater, I got my feelings on her, but she kept her hands to herself, not because she wasn't into me, but because she hesitated. After the date, I took her back to my apartment or condo as well as continued to gas her up about how fun it was hanging out with her (lie) how sexy she looked (she was pretty, but not that pretty), and how I didn't want her to leave (truth). After about forty mins, I had her bra off and my hands down her pants. She stopped me and told me she needed to go before she slipped up. I tried to go back to sweet-talking her right into staying, but to her credit scores, she did not give up. I had not been thrilled by her personality; I was excited by the prospect of having sex after seeing her half-naked.

A week of talking on the phone, flirting, and gassing her up had won her over, and she was willing to go all the way. I got head, had sex with her, and promptly got head one last time before telling her I was about to go to sleep. Asshole move, but this is how most men work when they come across a cute girl who isn't exactly intriguing. The average woman is unsure of herself when on a date with a guy she likes, which leads to awkward behavior and a corny vibe. Men don't want to hang with a cornball no matter how phat her ass is or how big her breasts are. Think if you do these things:

-Counter Conversation: Wait for him to speak, and also, you just react to his question with the answer and a dry followup about the same subject. Never stimulating your partner.

-Over Laugh: You don't have anything to add to what he's saying, yet don't wish to be peaceful, so you laugh more challenging than typical or laugh when nothing's that funny.

-Walk on Eggshells: You don't intend to say anything to upset this man, so you keep the conversation safe and unobjectionable. It's like putting someone whose best jokes have to do with homosexuals in a gay bar; they do not wish to offend, so they tone way down.

-Do Not Rape Me Body Language: You don't point your body towards him or inch close when walking. At dinner, you sit across, not next to him. Strolling to the vehicle with him, you keep your range.

These points are understandable when you're not acquainted with a person, but this isn't modesty ways to get a guy to see you as a sweet female, this is Ho Tactics to consume this guy active. Hos get real comfortable, real fast, and because it's such a different way for a woman to act on a date, men are taken off guard and easily satisfied.

Giving your business for a date without any intention of ever doing anything else, it's something that all ladies do. On that particular date, you likely did not give a fuck, so there was no counter discussion, you said everything. There was no over laugh because you didn't want him to think you liked him by over laughing. You did not walk on eggshells because this guy was much more like the homie than the royal prince lovely.

When it comes to body language, you most likely maintain your distance, but I'm sure you were relaxed, not bashful in concerns about how close you got to him. That man had not been a risk, so you did not act uncomfortable. In response you weren't seen as corny, you were viewed as the fun, somewhat goofy, the girl with excellent conversational abilities, which clown is probably still trying to take you out once again. You need to be able to be that comfy with men that are champions.

√ Kissing As A Reward.

Some women do not like kissing unfamiliar people, and that's easy to understand. Still, if you reject to reward his actions with love, it will make him get the feeling that you're just placing on a front and that lack of attraction will leave you dead in the water. Be prepared to kiss, but allocate it.

One girl also told me she kisses men; she doesn't like it because she does not want to be discourteous and change away. The first date, if it goes well, must end with a kiss, no tongue, short.

The second date you need to go French and kiss the fuck out of him, once more, don't get into a make-out session like an intoxicated blonde during homecoming. Before you say goodbye, give him another kiss, but this time, you should start and pull him in. When it's time to stop kissing, drawback as if you don't want to stop, but you're a good girl, so you have to quit.

This seduces his body and makes him instantaneously hard. You need his cock to be difficult; it's the last objective before you end the night. Kissing, rubbing his trousers, it's all a seduction plan to get him coupling you with love. As you move forward, kiss him like that when he does something you like, and also train him only to expect that level of kissing as a reward. He doesn't kiss you even if he wants to kiss. You're not a teen in love; you're softening him up for the hustle, so maintain your kisses on a limited lock up until he knows that he doesn't get sweet until he makes you smile.

√ C.L.I.T.T (Call. Pay attention. Overlook. That. Text).

It might be two days between dates or an entire week, but this is where women generally lose a guy's passion even after a suitable date—waiting for him to call, being afraid to call him first, texting, and not taking every one of this things is an item of worry. The most admirable feature of Hos is that they are just like Spartans when it involves tossing caution to the wind and taking control of their fate. Spartans call when they want because they made a connection and didn't need to play games. Hos call because they can't get paid with a dry phone. Same confidence, but they exist on different moral plains.

After you wow him on the first date, call to check him out the following evening if you have not heard anything. Men typically have a policy that you call a girl a day or more later on, but girls today overthink and get paranoid when they do not get a call or text 12 hrs after some younger guys contact the same night because they know how now women think. Regardless of how he responds, fast or slow—he wants you! Don't wait on him to hit you up like some scared little girl, initiate. Late at night is perfect because it catches him winding down and vulnerable. Call and thank him for taking you out, throw out some inside jokes, whisper about how you were daydreaming about kissing him earlier, and compliment his lips. If you do these things, his dick will be harder than finger wave gel. He now wants to know what every man wants to know, "when can I see you again?"

Do not react and be submissive this time and let him arrange the date. Unless he has something intriguing turning up like an honors dinner, show tickets, or some formal occasion, keep him at night. You're active, you have a life, tell him the weekend break may work, but you'll need to let him know. This keeps him starving. You refuted him seeing you, however just after you rode his penis about daydreaming about this kiss. You're challenging a man where most women toss themselves; he knows that you want that prick, but he just can not reach you. Therefore, he will relocate heaven and also earth to make Friday, Saturday, or perhaps Sunday work as your following date night. This is all happening because you're always much better at luring a male over the phone than via text.

√ Excuses Excuses.

Are you a lady that can say, "No, not tonight?" Can you quit on your own in the center of kissing? Can you stand your ground when a man is asking to take you back to his place, begging to sleep at your place, or offering to rent out a resort so you will not have to drive in bad weather? This is the part where you will be examined, so bear in mind how to fight with spontaneous thoughts that may put you in endangering situations. After the first date, a man will not wish to go out again, but he does so he can get closer to sex. After the second date, a guy will want sex, so he will always try to maneuver it to intimate areas. It's like drawing teeth, but a man will certainly not whine directly about taking you out, he will just go the detour and think of other ways to see you.

House dates, house-party, kickbacks, or pop up visits. In a man's world, s the same as going on a date because he's spending time, and that's what women who are looking for love need to see, that he's going to spend time. Of course, it's a trap, and men end up isolating these women and having sex after a few weeks. This is the world that basic bitches have created, not Hos. Basic Bitches are afraid to turn a man down because they don't want to be seen as mean

or uninterested. A Ho doesn't give a fuck about the way she is perceived, because she knows he wants her pussy, she's virtually put in in his face. Even if a man is annoyed with dating, he will continue to entertain the things she wants to do because she's not going to bend and fall for come and have fun.

Get like these Hos, and be comfortable with the words, "not tonight." You are not going to lose his passion since he still wants to fuck you, and as importantly, he delights in hanging out with you. If you were to have sex with a guy and afterward spend Monday-Friday, saying you do not intend to come and watch Ride Along, he's likely to call the following girl and put her over you.

It's not about how you make justifications, don't obtain caught up in having great reasons, fuck the ideas, be able to get the factor throughout that you do things on your time. Men hate when they can't have their way, yet hate is only frustration mixed with interest.

√ Tell Don't Ask.

Hey, they're having a white wine tasting uptown, let's go. By asking if he's "right into it" or "complimentary," you've already fucked on your because you don't seem sure if you even want to go. If you sound indecisive or placement yourself as a timid asker, then a male won't feel cynical about coming up with something that he wants to do instead, such as Dave & Busters or going over to his good friend's place to smoke and drink.

Shooting a guy down most times with your justifications about not being able to hang out makes him hard up. Now, he has to see you because he has to confirm to you that he is a boss, and also break you down like all the rest. As soon as you finally appear with a program that lets him see you again and potentially makes love, he will be down for anything. You have taken advantage of, you have power, and he goes to the grace of your demands. Use this power to go areas that you intend to go, that advantage your goal, and keeps you out of situations where you may endanger your discipline.

CHAPTER SEVEN

How to Fall in Love the Hos Way

The sexual destination is a shallow desire, which is why men weary so promptly after checking you off their breast it open container checklist. As a woman, you might be confused as to why men invest so much of their waking life attempting to get something that isn't even that serious. The same factor restaurants can bill $90 for a steak and build their business around the truth that they have $90 steaks. It's the allure of something more substantial and also far better. Intending to make love with various kinds of women is the itch that can't be scratched. He's never had a girl with D mugs, has never had a girl with A cups, has never had a Spanish girl, has never had an Arab girl, has never had a girl with all-natural hair, has never had a girl keeping that Cassie side cut spunk taking place-- men are in awe of anything that looks various and can't wait to experience it!

Old pussy merely tastes like new pussy; it feels better than fresh pussy, however like the guy that excitedly books to try that $90 steak, men have a burning need to try out new women-only because it's on such a high stand. Your pussy is the lure, and the method you seduce and flirt will undoubtedly increase you to that tall stand. However, those things do not assure shopping sprees or condominium down payments. The deep desire that makes you various from the typical pussy is love. Men fall in lust quickly, but they fall in love quicker if you recognize how to press the right buttons.

Take a guy that has a little sister; he will certainly do anything to make sure she's taken care of and that she's not being taken advantage of by men like him. Men are protectors by nature, it's in the male's DNA to hold down the fort, yet it's not home that makes him so caring, it's the love of being needed by someone special to him.

Take the family out of the formula; men still take specific women under their wings. Every guy that I've ever known has had a "sister" that had not been closed with him. That relationship was other, and sincere close friends weren't allowed to chat with his play sister, outside guys had actually to be authorized, and anytime she was in need, he did what he needed to make her satisfied. When their partners notify, bitter women who have never experienced this degree of spiritual male love typically change their nose up and boyfriend inform them about little sis

These women just see a man/woman partnership that's not developed on family, so it has to be sexual. Not every guy wants to fuck his play sister, yet the kernel of romantic love is at the origin to keep you in my pocket and secure you," conditional and also self-centered love.

Similarly, men love their play siblings; they fall in love with Hos. They give that sisterly love where they respect him, they need him, and they value him for assisting these women and represent that "Be My Daddy" sex-related dream. Daddy's gone, so Big Brother is there to safeguard her heart and also promote her desires, however at the core is the truth that unlike actual family, he can have her sexually. A Ho makes it clear that she is not his lady, but she also makes him feel as if she comes from him. No other guy is as ingrained in her heart as he has become, and that emotional possession makes her unique. The one Ho Tactic that will undoubtedly solidify your relationship past flirting and attracting, it's everything about being reliant like a little girl and making him feel as if he's your protector.

Hip Hop has promoted this, "You can't save a Ho," or the "Captain Save-A-Ho" rhetoric, but the truth is most of the guys rapping about not loving Hos are obsessed with them. A man with money or status treasures a girl that he can trip with, who doesn't bring romantic stress, and who always makes him feel like the only man in the world when they are together. That's the emotional jackpot; he doesn't have to commit to something scary or grow up and take on responsibility like marriage or a long-term relationship. This Ho is a friend, a confidant, a lover, and best of all, she doesn't put any pressure on him. Real women could never be happy with that self-centered role in a man's life, but Hos are built for concubine life.

When a female like that needs assistance with a bill, have it in mind that to go on getaway with him, or needs a pair of eight hundred dollar shoes to match the dress she just bought or it's going to spoil her evening, that man will go into large sibling mode. He looks after that female, not like it's his spouse, but like she's his defenseless little sibling. Men love Hosbecause unlike normal women, they do not howl, "I don't need any kind of guy," they press him tight and also say, "I would not know what I would do without you." That feeling of real gratitude, if it is sparked by what he does for her, is a real feeling, it is genuine love, and it finishes a man on the inmost degree.

Ladies often tend to drop into two classifications, either an independent female that does for herself or a lady that spoils a male because that's how you were raised to be. Men do value those women, they marry them, they like them, but they hardly trick on them.

Many of you reading this have boyfriends or husbands that don't buy you shit, but you know they have it to spend.

Your guy is more likely to deceive on a Ho or his "younger ones" before he ways on you, a loyal woman that gives him endless love. A man is comfortable in that duty to the factor that he neglects that you are still a female that needs to be treated like a princess now and then. Trophy wives, as well as Hos, usually have one significant thing in common, they need that man, they are reliant on that guy, and also they stroke his ego in a way that plays to his fraternal caring side and his savage sexual wish.

Girlfriends can't compete with Hos because they are carrying two exclusive skills. Girlfriend wishes that he will care for her, yet doesn't expect it, whereas a Ho sends to a male and pleads.

The open mouth is the one that is feed. Read this over and over once more until you recognize this as the nature of every man. When they, you were looking for the solution to why men take care of Hos

can locate women that will certainly do what they want for cost-free, well there it is.

Hoping Up

You do not need to be an actress or have some awful story that makes this man see you as a roaming

Many women go via unfortunate breaks up, childhood years drama, and things that have specified that they are. To make this man depend on you, you have to give him something worth thinking about.

It's like applying for a scholarship or trying to be admitted to the right college; there is always an essay that states why you deserve it on a personal level. This trick may fund your business, your lifestyle, or your next two automobiles, so you must give him a factor to fall for your spirit. Men love poor women attempting to be good or great girls that are one-step far from relapsing. Every woman has a story to tell, yet let's ensure it hits the right notes that will make a brutal man intend to invest in you emotionally.

√ Carve Out Your Territory

Weak women never know when it's right to call a guy, they text like mad, and date as if they do not want to interrupt a man's regularly scheduled life. They do these things because they are worried to be known as clingy, but by trying to get in where they fit in, they become slaves to a man's way of life and when a man knows that you are ready to be accommodating he will certainly exploit that at every turn. A guy such as a lady will want to call her every time, drop texts in the morning, and always been a phone call with her.

I don't care if you are unemployed and doing nothing than waiting for your favorite TV show to come on, or if you're busy working and going to school—you need to be viewed as active, but always have at least an hour for him each day. That hour tells him that you care and that you are invested, but it also demands that he must be available or he'll miss out that day. People in Long Distance Relationships do similar things to keep the spark going, but they stay on the phone all night trying to compensate for not being able to see each other for a long time.

√ Secret Swap

Some men are electric motor mouths and can not hold water, but if you mount what you have to say as if it's exclusive and no one knows it, then he can't talk on it. If it were to trickle, just you and he know about it so that he would fuck himself over, and also he's not going to do that while he's still gaining from you. Men aren't ready to share because they've been burnt by women that crossed their fingers and completely dried snitched to the world.

Hos are remarkable secret keepers that make them like specialists to many men. Of all the events that have broken in the media, some of the outcomes of a woman are snitching; it's circumstantial evidence or man sloppiness that discovers what that female wouldn't have told. If a man is likely to be deceiving you, spoiling you, or funding you, he's not going to let the world know. What he provides for you remains in between both of you. To get to that level, you need to confirm your trustworthiness early. When he asks what you say, your friends don't respond like a happy bitch, "I told them we went out to a dinner that you order for me at restaurants, that you're so sweet ..." No, bitch. You tell them nothing and educate him from the dive, "I'm not a bird that requires to boast, I such as to keep to myself.".

Let's say you were virtually molested when you were nine by a neighbor, yet you got away. Tell him how that still makes you feel, how you can't allow your guard down, and that you feel like you need to get it out, but you have not felt this comfortable until now. Don't push him for his tricks, given that if there is anything he wants to tell you, he does not have to stress about judgment or you bringing it up, because you would not want him to be that way with your secrets.

√ Lift The Sanctions.

Up until this point, I've told you to beware of the house dates, nightcaps, or pop-ups that men use to force women into sex. To prove that you're not a huge cock tease, start bringing the guard down.

Do welcome yourself over to his place.

Don't stay the night.

Do let him visit.

Don't let him hang around for longer than an hour chilling.

Open your world up to him, but don't let him get comfortable to the point where he thinks you will have movie nights or that he can come to see you with a pizza instead of taking you out. You have proven this man as having trick potential, but he's not a fool. If he sees an opportunity to slack, he will kick his feet and set his phone to your Wi-Fi network as if he plans to be over there often.

Take sex outdoors hangout. If you discuss it, it isn't to safe time; it's to talk about something that's bothering you or that you do not want to go over on the phone. When you're alone, and he's touching you and vice versa, let him get a little feel on, as well as the other way around, but bring it back to what you wanted out of the visit. Lounge with him, put your ass on his lap, give him a shoulder rub, but this isn't "boo time," it's putting in job to confirm that you're slowly yet definitely allowing him inside your world. The permissions have been lifted; however, the limits will be the same. Be disciplined and don't succumb to him wishing to give you head, or him begging for a handwork, that's too close for comfort. Make these brows through short, purposeful, and leave him wanting more. He would want you to come back again and do that the next evening if you jerk his prick after a visit. If he eats the box, he's going to expect that going forward. Don't go down that road. He needs to be tough and randy every time you leave him, which ensures that he will proceed to take you where you intend to go and get you the essential things you want. In his mind, he's one first date far from having you, and you should keep that fire burning.

CHAPTER EIGHT

How to Flirt with him without Being Obvious

Men have a tendency to be attracted in and also drawn to women they can flirt with.

At the same time, they are turned off by women who flirt aggressively and show their noticeable attraction because they don'tlike to feel they have made the first move.

All you need to do is make the guy assume he's making the first move when you're the one doing it, and no, winking at a guy is not teasing. It's a way to make him think you have a nerve injury.

Seems complicated?

Well, it's not as complicated as you think.

Just how to Flirt with a Guy Without Being Obvious

Knowing how to flirt with a guy subtly, will undoubtedly get you his interest and his (unchecked) destination in the direction of you-- before he even knows why.

Right here are the most effective means to get a guy's attention-- in any type of situation:

1. Eye Call

Of all the body language means to flirt with a guy, this seems obvious, but I'll bet you're not knowledgeable about the powerful impact of a long-staring kind of eye contact.

Stare at him until he knows and makes eye call with you when you're trying to get a guy's attention.

But:

Do not look away when he does!

When his eyes meet your own, keep gazing deeply into his eyes and grin a little smile.

This is the best way to flirt without being evident.

If you are now talking to the guy-- keep eye get in touch with as high as you can.

As you pay attention to what he states, search in his eyes, and do not quit. After a couple of minutes, he will feel like you are looking into his soul.

Flirty truth or dares are a fantastic way to flirt without exposing your attraction towards him.

2. Find Out His Passion

This refined way of teasing calls for a few minutes of thinking.

If you now know some things about your crush, utilize them to strike up a discussion.

As an example:

If you know he such as music, or some kind of sports-- find means to get him to talk with you about it.

If he like music, start a conversation about a concert you want to attend if it's football-- comment about the last match that was in the news.

If you do not know anything regarding him, check his sneakers, his T-Shirt, whether he has jewelry on him, anything that can be a discussion starter.

When I was single, I saw a charming guy on a trip to Los Angeles. I could see from his T-shirt that he is a band.

I was sitting one row in front of him, so I started playing with my Ipad, and delicately stood up and walked around with it then returned to my seat after he saw me, two minutes later he asked me about what I'm listening to. We spent the whole trip talking and went out for a few dates in L.A.

This is an effective flirting method you can use with any man, without making any kind of "move" and without even having to make eye contact.

3. Use Your Hair

Like this, but without the evident "turn and smile."

Men love it when girls run their hands with their hair.

The next time you're speaking to your crush, casually run your hand through your hair (and also smile if its right then). Or put your hair behind your ears to show off your pretty face.

This will reveal him your self-confidence, while still being "girly" and vulnerable-- Two things a guy can no resist!

4. Compliment Him Over Text (The Right Way).

Men, much like us, ladies, like to get adorable praise.

Make sure you compliment him about it if you like something regarding a guy.

He will undoubtedly love it that you observed something special about him, and also if you notice something that isn't so obvious (like his looks, as an example)-- even better.

Whatever you do, do not fake it.

Guys will notice fake praise and translate it as a miserable effort to flirt boldly, which is not what we're trying to do.

For instance:

 I will not compliment a guy about his looks (also apparent), but I would compliment his sense of humor if he has one

5. Accidental/Casual Pressing.

When a female that flirts with them all of a sudden (and gently) touches them, guys avoid a beat.

The only areas "permitted" and recommended are his arms, his shoulder or his back.

It makes them feel comfy and desired, and much more importantly-- it makes them available to you when they speak to you and also encouraged to flirt with you additionally.

Do not get his arm and tell him how big his muscle mass is. Nope.

As an example:

Subtle touching is leaning against him and putting your cheek on his shoulder for a split second while you laugh from one of his jokes.

How to Flirt with a Guy at the office.

Walking with a guy you like gives you an incredible advantage.

You get to see him every day, and you already have work in common?

Here are simple ways to flirt with your crush at the office:

-Raise your eyebrows discreetly when you take a look at him and smile.

-Touch him quietly (a pat on the shoulder)-- when you have a chance.

-Praise him on his work, or the way he treats other work colleagues.

-Show him your fun side, or something funny or silly when you're around him.

Use a "work-excuse" to message him after work hours.

Eighteen Ways to Flirt Without Being Slutty.
-Compliment him.

A woman compliments a man on something she finds eye-catching is very sexy without being symptomatic-- as long as she concentrates on his PG features.

"When you give a compliment, it shows that you are self-confident enough to make somebody feel good. This is not just making the guy feel less intimidated by you, but your evident confidence also makes you more appealing.".

-Smile.

It's secure, reliable, and any girl can do it!

" Smiling is the most convenient means to flirt," says Lieberman. "It's assured to make you look like the most prettier, and you don't have to plan for it firstly. An additional benefit to a smile is that it's non-committal. You can be flirting with him, or you can be keeping in mind something funny that someone said to you earlier in the day. So you don't have to be humiliated if he does not flirt back.".

-Give him openers for conversation.

Make it simple for him to speak with you by having a few subjects in mind that will get the discussion bubbling. You can discuss the place where you're, the beverage you love-- just anything that he might chime in on.

"Many guys get stuck in knowing how to start a conversation without looking dorky or smitten," says Lieberman. "So, if you give him an opening, he'll feel less on the spot and appreciate the encouragement."

Touch him.

A tap on the arm to buttress your point will do. (Conserve his inner upper leg after you've known much about him.).

" Flirty touching is a wonderful indication that you are into a man," says Sadie Allison, M.D."Yet keep it clean, so he doesn't get the wrong side of your light love.

Touching the face, arm, or hair is ok. A brush on his upper body could be ok too-- just been the stubborn belly!".

-Make eye call-- then avert.

" Making eye call and holding it for some seconds much longer than an informal look creates him to take notice of you and start to question what you might have meant by that," says Lieberman. "It's the great 'silent flirt' that can make him wish to know extra.".

No need to wink or lick your lips (ew!)- A simple look will do.

-Be expressive.

Catch his eye by being the sort of lady who isn't scared to rise and dance or remain seated and show her viewpoints.

" Showing a man that you are bold in your feelings about life can capture his attention and make him wish to get to know you," says Lieberman. "Men don't like women who are dull, inactive, or stale. Express on your own, and he'll wish to engage with you.".

Turn your hair.

" If you don't know it, flipping your hair is a traditional sign that you're flirting," says Lieberman. "It worked in sixth grade, and it will still work for you as a grown-up lady.".

Men discover the womanly elements of your appearance irresistible, and also there's nothing like the reliable toss of your hair to pique his interest.

-Tease him.

Another thing to borrow from the 6th quality? Be a little mean. Men love to be teased-- simply make sure that you try not to come off as rude.

" A well-placed barb that reduces his puffery can be effective," says Lieberman. "But, you need to be able to stroll the fine line between showing him that you're creative and not daunted, without harming his feeling. Men like an intellectual obstacle, but remember they have delicate egos that bristle at excessive mockery.".

-Be a real girl.

As opposed to what you might think, you don't need to be "one of the individuals"-- actually, be just the opposite!

" While it's great to have a 'gamine' up your sleeve for the fun sporty stuff you may do with him later, when you're new and just in the flirting stage, keep it fun and comfortable," says Dr. Allison. "Men are attracted to the womanly qualities of a lady and will make more seriously as a potential mate when you exhibit that. Plus, it will show him you'll know how to act app

-Ask him questions.

" Asking question shows you're interested in knowing him better," says Allison. "Noting on what he tells you is better and shows you're listening to what he's saying.

-Suggest hanging out.

A flirty way to ask for a date without actually proposing is to recommend doing something related to a topic you've just talked about. Like, if he said he only went snowboarding tell him you're interested in learning how.

" Lots of people speak, but many don't pay attention," says Fulbright. "He'll appreciate that you truly process what he says, and that is crucial enough to remember.".

-Raise something from the information

Okay. Do not be an existing occasions geek or Bachelorette-loony regarding this but request his point of view on something in the "news" or in popular culture that he could not have actually missed out on unless he lived under a rock.

" This shows you care regarding what he thinks," says Allison. "It's a terrific method to flirt andgives him a chance to have fun being around you. Know his thoughts, even if you do not agree. And make sure not to barge in with your own opinion, hindering his. Keep the conversation mutually specific. Stay away from slutty by not discussing sex-- in any way."

-Be open

When you have inviting body language-- looking friendly and cozy-- he'll find you far more approachable.

" Open body language is inviting and sends the appropriate message, so he knows you're into him," says Allison. "Subtle openness like loosened arms (never fold them), a lot of eye-contact, giggles, and grins to his comments are all good. Just don't take it much, like leaning in showing bosom, or not resting like a lady."

Be wanted

Use your powers of destination to get the interest of other men in the room. No-- do not construct with them. Just see to it he understands various other men notice you, as well.

" Being wanted by other men is a healthy and balanced addition to your overall flirt result," states Allison. "When you bring yourself well, hold your head high with confidence and also safety, it's extremely eye-catching to men. Add a hot outfit that's well-created to the mix, and there'll be no leaving you! When you notice eyes scanning you from across the area, just do not be shocked. When a guy observes other men curious about his warm date, it guarantees him he's got a good catch. He'll feel proud, and also, he'll want you a lot more."

Dancing with him

" Dancing is sensual in nature, allowing you to give hints of what's to share as well as come just how much you desire him without throwing on your own at him," says Yvonne K. Fulbright, Ph.D., writer of Sultry Sex Talk to Seduce Any Lover. "He can likewise really feel literally near to you, in a manner that will certainly have him desiring a lot more."

But no Humpty dancing, please.

Mimic his movements

When you mirror the activities of someone you're interested in, it sends out the signal that you're on the same wavelength. For beginners, try refined moves like sitting in the same setting that he is.

" This is the supreme flattery," says Fulbright. "And too much of the processing happens on a subconscious level, making us like people who picture us more."

-Ask him for assistance

There's no better way to make a guy feel wanted than to request his assistance with something-- even if you know you might do it yourself!

" It is great to be wanted and handy," says Fulbright. "It's a fantastic vanity stroke and shows that you think of him."

-Radiate self-confidence

" Self-confidence can be such an aphrodisiac when carried out in a real-- not look-at-me-- way," says Fulbright. "People glow when they feel good about themselves, and also, that's just attractive!"

Eight Ways That Come Across Needy Flirting is not as difficult as one might think it is.

He is smart, hilarious, captivating, and every little thing you have ever wanted in a man. You are not sure whether he likes you the same way.

Given, he associates you usually, sends you witty and cute messages often, and also got you a sweet bar that one time at the mall. But is that because he likes you or is it because he finds you a fantastic friend? There are only one means to discover.

You have got to flirt with him.

Flirting is not as difficult as you think it is. And, it's more or less having fun with your main man and letting him know you are interested than exciting him.

Believe it; once you master it, it will undoubtedly end up being a force of habit to you. You would certainly be able to attract almost any type of man on this planet. Not that you want any man. You just want that particular person!

To help you get there-- charm your main man-- we have placed with each other a checklist of 8 ways to flirt with him without being obvious and also eight ideas that can make you come across clingy.

Believe it; you don't want to be caught doing the latter!

> **Not Apparent: Smile And Wave At Him When You See Him**

Have you ever seen a kid smiling at you and felt a smile break out on your face also? You can not help but respond to that innocent look of happiness.

That's what smiling does to your man also.

The next time you meet him, smile and also wave at him with true love. You will see him inviting you back with a huge grin too.

Believe it; nothing is as contagious as a smile. (Maybe bacteria, but this is a flirting point of view, not a science lesson!).

Simply note: your smile needs it to be real for it to work its charm. Because all humans have a built-in fake sensor, it's. So, it will not help your situation if you are pissed off at him but greet him with a weak, plaster smile!

> **Clingy: Hug Him Longer Than It's Polite When You Meet.**

We recognize you have dropped head-over-heels for him. Your friends know you have lost head-over-heels for him. And also there's a high possibility that he knows you have fallen head-over-heels for him!

How can the man not when your feelings are all over the place whenever you are around him? And, there's that awkward thing you do by finding justifications to hug him regularly. That as well, longer than it's considered healthy!

Believe it; it's the neediest thing any individual can do when they have a major crush on somebody.

Not that we condemn you for doing it. We had all devoted such roguishness in the name of flirting when we were eco-friendly in the game. Just quit from right here on, and you would be good to go.

> ➤ **Not Evident: Hold His Gaze When You Are Talking To Him**

The eyes are the homegrown windows to the spirit. No wonder we are not comfortable checking out people's eyes for long when we speak to them. However, that's precisely what you need to do when you want to flirt with him discreetly and let him know you are interested.

Besides, don't you feel an added zing in your heart every time his eyes meet with yours?

When you hold his gaze during your discussions, you would be doing the same to him.

It's a subtle body-language cue that tells him that you are paying attention to him with rapt focus. That you think his words are outstanding and the discussion is critical. And, holding someone's look means bold self-confidence. And self-confidence is extremely eye-catching!

➢ **Clingy: Ask Him What He Thinks About Your Outfit.**

Please don't do this.

You could assume it's cute and forward when you ask him what he thinks about your dress, but in truth, it means instability.

The fact is, women that are certain about their appearance, their hair, and their outfit never ask men for praises in "subtle" ways like this. It's because they do not need appreciation to increase their self-image. They already know they look incredible, and if compliments come to their ways, they just happily accept it.

If you want to impress him, impress yourself. Put on something attractive.

> ➤ **Not Noticeable: Whisper In His Ears When You Are Out With Him In A Public Place.**

The best thing about this tactic is that it brings the two of you closer but does so in a classy manner.

Since crowded locations tend to be somewhat noisy, the two of you will either have to shout to be listened to the racket (not recommended!) or flex so you can whisper your conversation into each other's ears.

The last develops a sense of affection because whispering brings a person more profound into your private room.

You can be sure that this method will certainly bring the two of you more closed even after you have walked out of the congested situation and don't need to breach each other's personal space anymore.

Just now, you would not mind doing it anyway.

Needy: Whisper In His Ears For No Reason.

The reason why the previous strategy works yet this does not is that, in a crowded area, you don't have an option but to murmur in each other's ears. But when you are the only two people in a park and can quickly hear each other from some range, deliberately dipping close to whisper in his ears would promptly trigger him to regurgitate his guard. He has not invited you into his private room!

Keep in mind: this strategy is about flirting with him when you are not sure whether he likes you or not. Since if the two of you are now close, and you think he likes you, this technique would certainly not work so misplaced.

> ➤ **Not Apparent: Slowly Shift Your Hair From One Shoulder To The Other While Talking To Him.**

Below's a reality nobody can refute: ladies have beautiful hair! Since they clean it regularly and make an initiative to keep it shiny and healthy, primarily.

That's the reason he loves it when you run your fingers through your locks or play with a hair while you speak with him. Nothing sets off his creative imagination better than this natural, lively, but powerfully-feminine move!

Another time you are having a real conversation with him, gently move your hair from one side of your head to the other and then tuck in the roaming strands behind your ear. It's one of the simplest means you can obtain him to start thinking about you as the one!

> ➤ **Clingy: "Accidentally" Rest Your Foot Against His Again Even Though He Shifted His Away A While Back**

Here's a basic body-language example for you: if someone allows you to rest on your foot against their own when they accidentally end up touching, it suggests they have an interest in you and do not mind you trespassing in their private area. Yet if they move their foot away, it means they are not comfortable with you (if you have just met this person) or are not thinking about you romantically (if the two of you have hung several times already).

When the last occurs when you are with your main man, regardless of how much you may like him, do not try to rest your foot against his again! You would be disrespecting his private room and also will depict yourself as clingy.

> ➤ **Not Apparent: Touch A Finger To Your Lip While Thinking**

Touching a finger to your lip is among the most powerful flirting methods. It can generate passion in him promptly! Utilize this tactic intelligently and also modestly if you do not desire to make your interest in him extremely evident.

One right way of doing that is touching your lip in his presence while you are thinking something.

This gesture is all-natural, and also so does not arouse his uncertainty. It, however, conveys a message to his subconscious mind-- that you are a lady he might kiss one day if he asked you out.

This technique is like the modern variation of the "drop your scarf before him" technique that women used in the olden days. The idea is to put the idea of pursuing you in his head while making him think it was his idea always!

> **Deprived: Find Excuses To Pick Up Something On The Floor Infront Of Him Or Pull An Impromptu Yoga Pose**

We get it! You take pride in your physique.

Possibly it's because you have been operating at the fitness center frequently and have shed some added pounds, or perhaps it's because you were born with a supermodelesque body and intend to reveal it off.

Whatever your reason might be, do not draw this technique in front of him if you don't want to look clingy. Nevertheless, many people do not keep dropping their phones, cappuccinos, and tricks several times (please do not go down the latte!) in fifteen minutes!

Do it only once if you want to use this flirting method (it's one of the more interesting ones). That is, either drop your pen innocuously and after that pick it up while he's watching, or reveal that your muscles are feeling cramped from resting for as long and afterward do some regular yoga exercise stretches!

 ➢ **Not Obvious: Compliment Him About Something Specific**

You probably do not know this, but men love praises (real ones, that is) just as much as you do. The only distinction is, society thinks that women need to be matched while men do not.

Just keep these points in mind before you end up devoting a praise faux pas.

One: compliment his character, not the activity. If he helps an older woman cross the street, tell him he is a kind man because he did so.

Two: be extremely specific. So, don't simply tell him he is cute. Inform him you find him adorable because he opened the door for you.

And three: don't compliment his looks. Because if he is good-looking, he has heard it many times already!

➤ Needy: Pinch His Cheeks Or Jaw When You Praise Him

When we are incredibly crazy with somebody (or have a significant crush!), we can not help but want to touch them as much as we can. It's a personal demand, so do not feel odd about it.

Having stated that, if you keep finding reasons to pinch his cheeks or touch his jaw early on in your interaction, you will just come off needy.

Believe it, you could assume it's cute when you tell him he is tremendous and then pinch his cheek like a five-year-old, but he possibly will shift far from you soon reason being that you intruded in his personal space without his permission.

A much better idea is to slowly relieve him into being all right with your touches by cleaning your shoulder against his while you are strolling side-by-side or by holding his hand when you go across a busy roadway.

> **Not Apparent: Touch His Arm Or Shoulder Gently While Talking To Him**

This is a much more confident flirting strategy, but if done correctly will not excite anyone's uncertainty.

All you need to do is brush your shoulder against his every time and also after that as both of you stroll next to each various other and afterward gently touch his arm every single time you want to draw his attention to something you have observed going on.

Just keep in mind: every action of yourself needs to be all-natural; otherwise, it will become very noticeable to him that you are flirting.

That means, if you clean right into him, it truly needs to seem like you were looking in another direction; therefore encountered him inadvertently. Or maybe you found his joke funny and bumped his shoulder to show your appreciation.

Believe us, you will locate lots of methods to touch him naturally; you just need to get hold of the opportunity with confidence when it provides itself!

> ## Clingy: Exaggerate Your Actions and expressions Whenever He Is Around

Yes, we know you are delighted to see him, yet that doesn't mean you become a total clown when he appears! Peacocking like that is a giant giveaway that you are seriously in love with him, which's the easiest way to lose his interest, given that it would make him feel that he can have you without also putting in an initiative.

So, control your emotions anytime you are with him.

You don't require to be an ice queen (please do not repress your emotions entirely); just be at convenience as well as continue to be positioned. Men love women like that.

And, exaggerated expressions and activities, just to get his interest, always making you feel like a high-level dramatization queen. And good men usually are not attracted to that!

> ➢ Not Obvious: While Walking Away From Him, Turn Back And Smile

This is possibly the best flirty idea on this checklist. Because it's one of the sweetest and most remarkable methods, you can allow him to know you find him exciting and adorable without making it very noticeable.

So, the next time you state bye-bye, walk two steps away from him, then turn back as if you desire to catch one last peek of him, smile and wave at him, and afterward leave without looking back again.

Believe it; he will still be thinking concerning this adorable moment even after he has gotten home.

Just don't do that often. Two times is more than enough, although I think once is perfect.

> ➢ **Clingy: Scribble Your Phone Number On A Paper And Then Kiss It Before You Give It To Him**

This set is so needy; it's hilarious. And also, we most definitely do not want you to be the butt of the joke. So, avoid this one if you do not want him to laugh at you nervously as he takes the paper and afterward never calls you once again!

It's because when you kiss the paper, it informs him instantaneously that you are interested in him and that he does not require to make any even more initiatives to thrill you. And men tend to shed passion genuine quickly after that, which is something you don't want.

If you want to give him your number, do so with confidence. Perhaps even say something in the long run, like, "I typically don't give my number to people, but you seem very interesting." It would all at once be a compliment, and also an obstacle has given that it would certainly tell him you appreciated the conversation with him, yet he still hasn't surprised you completely.

When it comes to teasing, it's always best to allow his creativity to do most of the work and still make him feel like he is the one chasing you!

CHAPTER NINE

Flirting and Sexual Attraction Body Language Signal

In the game of sex-related journey, what you say isn't as almost essential as what your body states. If you are so great at silent speech, you can say so much more with your body than words can ever do for you.

Here's just how it's done.

1. Triangulating Eye Contact

First, you need to accentuate yourself. That can be accomplished with adjusting the necklace, collar or earring, or flicking dust from your sleeve or shoulder, just to mention a few. After you catch his attention, hold his gaze for about three seconds, break eye contact downwards to take in the nose, lips, and chin.

Triangulating eye-contact connects the need to know the other person more thoroughly (and I am not speaking about "sex" people!). While men typically do not mind prolonged eye call with a strange woman (in fact they crave it specifically if she's stunning), women, on the other hand, tend to be instead aggravated by long stares of unknown men (also good looking ones).

Beware of cultural differences.

2. Eyebrow Flash

Eye call with an eyebrow flash followed by a smile has an extra effective result.

Make eye call, hold his/her gaze for about three secs, and break eye call downwards (very quickly). As you look again, take note of the chin, lips, nose, and find your way up to the eyes. Add in the eyebrow flash and smile.

The message you are passing across is, "I was only respectful initially ... and now that I've taken a good look...OH-WOW!"

Shy people can do this a lot far better than the more aggressive type because nuance and discreetness comes to shy males and females naturally.

3. Eye Catching

When you have his interest and conversation is streaming, use your fingers to accentuate your eyes and to maintain his stare focused on you - as well as you alone. This is specifically crucial when the exchange is happening in confined or jampacked problems.

Discreetly touch your nose or gently scrub your cheek, making sure your forefinger touches the area around the outer edge of your eye; your other fingers pointing to the mouth area. This says, "See, we're having a discussion right here." To create excellent rapport, be sure to hold eye contact when the man is talking, after that as his or her gaze starts to roam, bring it back by directing his/her eyes to your eyes and also mouth area.

Another thing you can do is to hold your face in both hands with the chin resting on your palms and elbow joints on the table. Delicately stroke the area around the outer edges of both eyes with your index or middle finger; the other fingers somewhat spread out in a semi-circle around your face. This provides the illusion of a murmur or secret being shared. Very intimate!

And also, if you use glasses, gradually take them off, rub your eyes very quickly and also put the glasses back on. And do not jab your eyes red because the apple of your eye has his or her focus attracted the guy or stylish the other side of the space.

4. Sidewards Glance

This is best attained when leaving or when resting with your back, changed in the direction of the person you want to be attracted to. Gradually look back with partially shut eyelids yet drop the gaze after it has been noticed. This stare decrease should be brief. Search for triangulating your eye call starting with the chin, lips, nose, and working your way approximately the eyes. Smile.

Dampening the lips at the same time you drop the gaze increases sex-related tension.

For women, the sideways glance incorporated with a hair throws and parted lips can be useful. 5. The Leg Cross (women just).

Knit legs accentuate body poise and give the impact of high muscular tissue tone. Crossing and uncrossing legs while being loved by an interested male is a strong attraction signal, particularly when you simultaneously hold eye contact, tilt your head sideways, and also stroke or rub a knee.

The catch right here is that the type of men you are more than likely to attract with this action are horny men - yeah, the hit-and-run kind! Unless you genuinely know the guy and also have his statistics inspected out, keep both your feet on the ground - and together.

And if you're a pair or wed, these body language actions can work wonders for your sex-related chemistry. And when integrated with prolonged eye contact and fondling round objects like the stem of a white wine glass, straw, pen, pencil, or cigarette... Aiyaiyaiyiayai! Houston, We Have a Problem".

Not always. Directly, I do not believe that mechanical body language gestures, nonetheless smooth, straightforward, and flawless, can do anything for you aside from enhancing your confidence and obtain the sex-related power streaming in your body. Its the confident feelings originating from you that begin the sexual attraction. Body language can just get the currently existing sexual chemistry going. If you can make use of body language to cause a domino effect, you're halfway there!

And simple as it takes effort and strategy to be fluent in any language, you need the technique to be well-versed in body language. You can practice before a mirror or with the help of a helpful, good friend. You'll see that as you are much more well-versed in your flirting and sex-related destination body language, your self-confidence in yourself as a sexually appealing lady increases also.

The goal is not to become a body language expert yet to become sexually confident with the opposite sex. Just have fun with your sex-related being.

You can also use this knowledge to evaluate whether someone was flirting with you, checking on you, and attracted to you. Remember, body language is no precise scientific research.

6. Lively Touches.

If you're interested in a guy that appears reluctant to take things to the next level, a couple of well-timed, "unexpected" touches can make a big difference. This unlocks him to do the same, and it will make him feel more comfortable around you.

Make the touches discrete. When you praise something he's using, you can quickly touch it.

7. Show Genuine Interest.

Being an excellent conversationalist isn't about crafting creative phrases or showcasing your achievement. It's about being a good listener. He'll feel like the most crucial person in the area when you ask the right question and give a man your full attention. That is an addicting feeling, and it will undoubtedly leave him wanting more.

Be genuinely interested in him and his life. Without making it look like a meeting, ask about his family and his business. If he has any hobby you are not familiar with, ask for an explanation of how they work.

While he's speaking, be still and alert. When he stops, do not instantaneously release all the ideas you've been thinking while he was talking. It will make him feel like you're a lot more interested in your viewpoints than in his.

A reliable but basic conversational technique is to make use of the other person's name. Hearing your name from another person is like a psychological pull. Of course, going too far with this might slip him out a bit, yet using it moderately is a great way to build affection.

8. Be Innocently Seductive.

Being innocently sexy doesn't mean moving your darkest lipstick and most revealing attire. It's even more lighthearted and cheeky than that. Flirting properly is everything about the subtle cues. The guy will certainly notice them, yet it's not naturally apparent to any person passing by what is happening.

Playing with your clothing, jewelry, and hair will draw his attention to them. Running your fingers through your hair repeatedly. Attack your lip sometimes. When he's talking, do not hesitate to let your eyes wander from his eyes to his lips again and again. Lean in his direction when he's talking, like you're mindlessly attracted to him.

9. Finish the Conversation First.

Do not wait till you've run out of discussion ideas before you bail. Leaving while the exchange still really feels fresh and energetic will leave him with a positive impression of you. He'll be eager to see you once again and share them if he felt like he had more things to add.

When you're first getting to know somebody and are determined to be around them, this can be difficult to do. It's much far better than standing there until you run out of things to say and have to leave on an awkward or apathetic note. Leaving him wanting more is much superior to over-sharing on the first interactions.

Recap: How to Flirt Face to Face:

-Compliment and tease him- just don't overdo either.

-Smile-- and suggest it!

-Touch him playfully (don't be also hostile).

-Payrealinterest in what he has to say.

-Be innocently seductive. Don't be reliable, just give him signals of interest so he can go after other things.

-End the discussion first-- it's always best to leave him wanting more.

Flirting From a Distance.

Teasing from across the room can be hot and appealing. It can be with a guy you're currently interested in, or an attractive stranger you just found and want to know better, teasing from a distance gives him the thumbs-up to approach you and initiate some face-to-face flirting.

-Eye call

Eye get in touch with is the most noticeable method to flirt from afar. A guy will discover in his field of vision if you look at his way softer.

If he's interested, this will make him fascinated. It's another way to stay away from mistakenly looking at him for long.

-Smile

Pairing eye contact with a pleasant smile is like a perfect one-two strike. Besides walking straight up to him, there's very little you can do to make your feelings known.

Don't fall under the trap of thinking that a chilly, disinterested expression is appealing. A female playing hard to get is a tired technique that only a man who loves mind games will be turned on by her. This isn't the kind of guy you wish to date, so do not cater to that.

Also, if you do not get the possibility to smile straight at him, laugh a lot, generally, will certainly make you inviting and friendly.

-View your body language

Most of our interaction is non-verbal, which means you need to be paying attention to your body language. Standing rigidly with your arms securely gone across resembles a gigantic "STOP" indicator to any type of nearby men.

If you're a little timid and find it difficult to unwind, start keeping that winning smile. Take a deep breath and allow your muscular tissues to chill out. Keep your pose open and your chin up-- this shows confidence. Having fun with your hair is classic flirtatious body language.

Be where he is (without following him around).

Whenever you have the chance to move closer to him, touch it. Discretely finishing up in his primary area is a peaceful means to capture his attention and hint at your interest.

Make your means to it and get a drink if you see him standing near the bar. You can try "mistakenly" running into him heading there or back. See if there's any person you know standing near him, as this would be a solid reason to join them.

Don't stress yourself on this. Take action back if you've placed yourself in his path, and he's not doing anything about it. Either he's not interested, or he needs to be more positive in finding you. Do not do all the work on your own.

-Be certain.

There's no specific collection of actions that highlight the best way for flirting with a person. What helps one person may not help another. That's why one of the essential factors in flirting is self-confidence.

If you portray a carefree and fearless attitude, it will serve you well in any kind of flirty searches. Having a positive, energized disposition will attract men in regardless of what you're doing.

On the days where you find it challenging to be sure, just fake it. Going through the activities of a particular person will, at some point, end up making you feel like one for genuine.

Wrap-up- How to Flirt From Across the Room:

Make eye call- simply be careful not to look—blinking, making eye call with looking away.

Smile at him coyly from throughout the area, then avert.

Have open body language- try not to be stiff and shut off; this sends a "stay away" message.

Being in his closeness and after that, let him start the call.

-Be confident.

Flirting Via Text/Messenger.

Message him in feedback to something he posted.

Rather than passively "taste" something he publishes on social media, take the initiative and send him a straight message. This doesn't promptly betray your purposes, yet it can prompt him to flirt if he's interested.

You might message him sating, "Your canine is adorable. If he shares a video clip from a performance he went to, you can send, "Just saw your video from the concert last night.

One thing here is to add a minimum of one question in your message. It's harder for him to believe in what to say if you just send out a compliment or basic statement. By asking a question, you open the door to another conversation.

-Ask an interesting question.

Talking of the question-- don't ask bland ones. This is why many people give one-word actions to questions like that.

Dig a little deeper. Ask questions that need more than a "yes" or "no" answer. Do not just say, "Seen any kind of interesting movies lately?" Choose for an extra specific, "What's your favorite film and why?" With the first option, he can quickly say no, and the conversation is made. With the second concern, he needs to include something personal about himself.

An excellent topic to explore at the beginning is work/careers, family members, and pastimes. When you get to know him better, you can look into hopes, concerns, and big dreams.

-Do not send a barrage of messages.

Imitate his texting design for the very first little while. If he's sending messages that are 1 or 2 sentences, do not send him three paragraphs. It might be that he's obtaining warmed up and also not all set to claim a whole great deal. But he also might be signaling that he's not too eager to talk, which means you don't intend to be spending a lot in the discussion.

Never keep sending out texts if he isn't reacting. It's either that he's not his phone; in that case, no amount of question marks after your texts will make him respond much faster, or he's not right into it. Once you send a text, distract yourself with another thing as well as let go of stressing over when or how he will positively react.

-Image texts.

Photo messages are an enjoyable method to feel a lot more participated in what the other individual depends on. Stating that your pet dog looks adorable resting on your feet is never going to be as fascinating as sending out an image of the described sight.

Stand up to being as well symptomatic in your pictures (unless you individuals go to the stage). At the very same time, there's nothing wrong with ensuring you look your best in any kind of pictures you do send his method.

Bitmojis, gifs, as well as emojis, are all useful tools for crafting an amusing as well as a powerful message. Goofy gifs, mainly, can be uproarious when utilized as a reaction. If he tells you concerning something ridiculous that occurred at his task, you might send a gif of a favorite TV personality doing a face-palm.

Be a little symptomatic.

There are indirect ways you can show interest via text. Showing that you want you were with him instead of texting him is one of the very best choices. If he claims he simply whipped up some pasta for supper, you can state you want you were consuming that rather of whatever it is you're eating.

When he sends something adorable or amusing, you can say, "Well, thanks, you're now in charge of me smiling at my phone like a bonehead." An additional option would be, "Wow, I just grunted out loud at that.".

One means to be symptomatic is to mean things which can be perceived as attractive, without being outright. As an example, if you do not obtain a possibility to react to his message immediately, you could say, "Sorry, simply left the shower! Anyway -" That does not outright flirt. However, it's a scheming way to make him think about you being in the bathroom.

Open the door to take things off a conversation and personally.

You just wish to stay in the teasing over the message phase for so long. The good news is, there are countless opportunities to shrewdly mean taking things up a notch.

Say you 'd love to see it sometime if he informs you about something he got for his house. This likewise benefits when he discusses any animals that he has. Because all animals love you, you can joke that you're pretty positive you 'd win his pet dog over in a heartbeat.

If he asks a question that could quickly be a personal or lengthy answer, tell him that the reply is means to wish for a message, so you'll have to tell him in person sometime.

Movies and bands are great reasons to meet up also. Say it if a group you both like is coming to town. You can also discuss how you've been dying to see a particular film, and it shows this weekend.

Recap How to Flirt Via Text.

-Message him in reaction to something he posted.

-Ask interesting questions, i.e., not "What's up?".

-Do not keep pounding him with messages. Wait for a response first, and don't stress if he takes a while.

-Send out cute photo texts.

-Be a little suggestive- suggest that you wish you were with him instead of texting, but do this in subtle means.

-Open the door to take things offline and face to face.

Why Hos Usually Win with Flirty Body Signal

Hos win because they live an enviable lifestyle that many women wish they could emulate. Each person's definition of winning is different, and the place where many women wish they could win isn't financially. They want the three A's: Attention, Affection, and Appreciation. Whereas Girl B has functioned hard to reveal that man that she's truthful, nurturing, and his equivalent, yet can not get anything but assurances and penis. While I am sure this book will have lots of critics that misunderstand the motif of this book as something sneaky and deceptive; it is a lot more equipping than any of these, "Wait For God To Show You Mr. Right Blah This Too Shall Pass" teachings that would have you position your fate in the hands of men rather than use your brain in the same means men have been doing for centuries.

I see how the younger generation of men are coming of age with little to no regard for women because the message of cooking area bitch submission has many females submissive and docile. The supposed "New Niggas" do not see most women as smart, they see them as holes, and it's not merely men born in the late '80s or early '90s, the older generation of men are seeing how simple it is to change and scam women out of pussy also. Dating is bush West, and women are being wiped out like the Native Americans because they refuse to move forward with the times and use modern warfare.

What's happened there is an "Us versus Them" line drawn in the sand where women have ended up being so turned off by men's habits that they give right into anger and defensive debates about the duty of a male in their lives. I always listen to, "Maybe if men understood exactly how to appreciate a good woman as opposed to a poor bitch, kids would certainly be increased right" or "Tell these men how they ought to act because we're doing our part." Those mindsets are born from frustration. Women are revolted that men don't act the ways they are meant to behave. Meaning, if she treats him well and respectful, he must treat her the same. That will certainly not happen because men will always have alternate motives when selecting mates that have absolutely nothing to do with what a woman holds him down or is most devoted to! Rather than sitting back and seeing stunning women crumble because asshole after asshole declines or discards them, I needed to show in the most obvious way possible, exactly how any kind of female can win!

This book isn't just about getting anything from men; it's about getting everything from life. Yes, you and your best friend are independent women who don't need to mindfuck a guy because you are self-sufficient. I'll toast to that. You don't need to get spoiled or sponsored because you can treat yourself to a spa day or a handbag. I'll toast to that. Cheers all around because I love that "I'm both King and Queen" power. However, it would be foolish to ignore the truth.

The reality is, there are several degrees of female power, and you should not stop learning them since you are a web content career woman or married.

Someone told me early on in this process that she doesn't like the thought of women lying to men, and also that Ho Tactics are hazardous. I don't think such as the thought of men lying to women, yet guess what, all my male friends do it on a day-to-day basis. It's not about stooping to their level; it's about knowing that level to tap into this Ho power whenever you need it. Why should any woman want to tap into this Ho power when she can stay on the straight and narrow and be a phenomenal woman? The straight and narrow is failing! The most honest and loving women out there are being strung along because they are taught to pray on it instead of knowing why they are being hustled. I'm sick and tired of seeing single mothers who do everything right, then end up falling for players. I'm sick of seeing from women in their 30's that are still going after the commitment carrot from the same bum that's been looking out of their lives for many years because they do not think any man would want them at their age. There is more power to be gained back in friendships and marital relationships, even if you dip a little bit into the so-called dark side of Girl Power.

No problem the situation I mention for the need of Ho Power, there will be detractors who will feel I've gone too much because these methods do not mesh well with their weak bitch programs. A few of you reading this may be confused about if you must or should not apply these strategies. Those of you reading this book and realize the lessons will permanently change if you never draw a mark in your life. You will find a new level of self-confidence that will stun you.

This is your trip, no matter who shares it with you or criticizes you for it, you came to these web pages to discover something new, and also you have. It does not quite right here; you should keep reinforcing the lessons up until your confidence is untouchable.

Don't care if you are too soft to be a Spartan or too honest to be a Ho. This book is proof that you are willing to get your dream man any means you can get him attracted to you.

Eye Contact Flirting is the First Step to Making a Connection

Eye contact flirting is usually the first step to attracting a person of the opposite sex. You have to know the basics of flirting via eye contact.

When we consult with our mouth and listen to our ears, the mind is associated with the process. Eye contact is the language of the heart. As soon as we know the fundamentals and increase our reduced self-confidence after that, the heart can step in and understand the signals. This does not mean that we don't have to know what contact is informing us.

Eye contact flirting usually starts from across the area. We observe them from the various other sides of the space, and they see us. They glimpse your direction and also allow your eyes to get in contact. Frequently the most significant obstacle is to endure enough and certain sufficient not to move away when returning their eye contact. If we look at them and after that shyly turn away from them, we never can be useful in flirting.

Among the signals, we may receive from across the room is a sideways sight. This method is secure but subtle. This is done by making contact with their eyes after that averting a little after a short while. This is a similar gesture to turning to avoid eyes to eye contact, yet involves one person admiring the other after that holding eye contact for a short moment and after that discreetly moving their head to the side. This move is frequently used by women to send out the signal that they're interested.

The next I signal to be knowledgeable about, which commonly comes after the sideways glimpse, is the extended glimpse. In this situation, the lady makes eye contact with men then holds this for a more extended period and perhaps grins. This can be a strong declaration that is meant to transmit the idea that some attraction exists between both parties. Some shy people may do this in gradual actions until they feel comfortable and are sure to return the eye signal.

When you have made face-to-face contact, eye contact takes on a whole new stage. This stage involves more direct communication between the two of you. Typically by this stage, an interested person will give you a fierce look.

One more popular activity is the up and down daze. This is that "check him out" eye contact; this is typically done when passing each other in a room or corridor. This can be an invite to another communication. Once they have admitted the reality that they're interested in this check it out the gaze, then the rest of the process may move rather promptly. Keep in mind that to succeed in flirting, you should know and understand how to identify the signals that have to do with eye contact.

Enjoy Flirting By Using Just Your Eyes

Flirting is the initial stage of courtship. Trifling as it might seem, to flirt is a sexual act where a woman and a man, might begin to show their desire for each other. This spirited shot at love does not exist in all the cultures around the world; it is also part of the standard instinct of man and a few other members of the animal kingdom.

But let's restrict the conversation within the bounds of men. Data show that over 50% of one's impression concerning another person is based on the looks, faces, and body language of that other person. Currently, amongst these features, the eyes play the most significant duty in making or damaging your possibility to leave a long-lasting and attractive impression.

The eyes are the most expressive parts of the body. Have you ever discovered how to flirt with guys or girls as the situation may be, exclusively by eye contact?

Making eye contact with someone across the room is a good sign that you and the one that person you are gazing at are crushing and looking into each other. This is your very first form of interaction; the chance to say that you are interested in that person sans words.

- Repeated Glances To The Floor

Gazing downwards periodically during an eye call is an obvious way to show one's discreetness. This kind of eye gesture is arguably the peak of flirty actions as it can be considered the partner of blushing. Many guys and girls find that a lengthy straight eye contact populated with periodic downward glances can be a very attractive act of flirting.

- Proceeded Direct Eye Contact

It signifies that both your emotions for each other are high if you and the person you are looking at can keep extensive eye contact. In regards to teasing, this kind of stare can typically call forth big smiles and enhance your impulse to take the actions to exchange a few words and spend some intimate moments together.

- The Fan And The Eye Contact

If flirting were to be an art type, creating eye contact against the background of a follower covering the rest of the face might be considered the Mona Lisa of flirting. Fortunately, this method, so to talk, can only be used by women. A male holding a fan in his face and also doing the eye contact routine might send the wrong signal.

This flirting style goes back to the moment when women of high culture, no question was obliged to be traditional and were always accompanied by their chaperones. Instead of being entirely intimidated by the visibility of their companions-slash-guardians, those women had developed a way to communicate with the men of their dreams using eye contact and a follower. It is the eye contact that interacts, and the fan just operates as a cover-up.

Throughout the years, the fan and the eye call became inseparable tools for flirting. A communication code has been created using these two. For instance, to state that a lady loves his boyfriend, she just has to conceal her eyes behind an unfolded guy; on the other hand, jerking the amateur from one eye to the other announces that a lady is sorry.

CHAPTER TEN

Get Him in the Mood for Sex

Here's useful information for all the women out there-- men are pretty simple to seduce. Men are incredibly visual animals, and also the only means to make him entirely your own is by getting more creative with your flirting skills. What should you do to get him in the mood for sex tonight?

Show a little skin. That's right. Let's get technological in the meantime. Men love to seem some skin, and it will not harm if you do. Make it as subtle as possible as you can. A couple of body-fitting gowns would do. That's enough to get his hormonal agents raging and extremely turned-on in a couple of seconds.

As a lady, a typical man would expect that you 'd be smelling nice and pleasant all the time. It's an excellent aphrodisiac as well as the more you obtain better with him, allowing him to get a whiff of your perfume, the more he 'd want to be in bed with you sooner.

Obtain close and flirt. When out on a regular bar night-- it keeps you eye-catching and also enticing, flirting is your number one tool. Flirt as long as you can yet do not come off as somebody entirely cheap to get. Send out blended signals and take some time to tease his creative imagination. He'll wish for more all night long.

If you feel desirable and attractive, you begin to look the part too. Know how to blink him a few beautiful and playful looks, and also, men would be salivating after you.

Stare right back if he's blinking you some smiles and trying to make eye contact stare right back. That would get him all discharged up. Not all women are incredibly daring when it comes to flirting with men. The more you get dangerous and hostile, the more they would attack the lure. So keep eye contact with him at all costs.

So you would like to know THE secret? Yearning for more one on one action for two? Passing away to discover the simple steps on just how to get laid? Think it or not, it is very easy as one, two, three. Don't believe me? Keep reading my friend; keep reading.

The actual secret is that it is no secret. How? Its common area knowledge prepared in the appropriate order that gets you the final rating. You have to make it for the night you need. It has been sais that "cleanliness is next to godliness" and by George, you want to be adored tonight!

Shower, brush your teeth, comb your hair, shave (unless you maintain a facial rug...in such case, trim carefully), and by all means use deodorant. If you like, add one of the come hither body deodorants or cologne attracting to the opposite sex. Make sure you wear clean clothes and let's not forget what mother said always wear clean underwear! If you like, add one of the come hither body deodorants or fragrance appealing to the opposite sex. Get yourself in the state of mind, spirit, body, as well as mind to be the most beautiful view to the eyes of your prospects.

The next step is to scope out your surroundings. You've probably chosen a bar or club as your location of choice, and the probability of you meeting someone's standards is high. Whether or not he is your top pick is not relevant as you just want to get laid.

This can be anything from willful disregarding to a flat out pick-up line. Gauge the situation and choose what's right for you. As soon as you have him complete on interest, it's time to adopt a ball game! More than likely, you both have the same program. It's late; you're both out minus a "partner" and searching for a quick turn with somebody new. Shut the deal with an invocative proposal, and you've won the race.

How to Get Your Man in the Mood

A great deal of work goes into finding out exactly how to obtain women in the state of mind for sex, but what about the men? They are worthy of some play and indulging as well, so girls (and gents) it's time to learn more about your partner and also precisely how to get them in the mood so that you can have the deep or astonishing and enthusiastic sex you've always wanted.

-A Hot Shower

And I don't just mean the temperature. A hot shower soothes away aches and pains from a long day, and the warm water helps to lubricate massages. And also, being naked with each other in a steamy space is a fantastic means to get started. That knew that being clean could be so dirty?

An Erotic Massage

Does your man got back sore and 'crunchy' feeling (i.e., his bones and joints pop and breeze)? He'll value a sensual massage therapy on so many levels. Have him naked, and after that lie with his back on some pillows. Beginning at his ankle joints and knees and work your way through his abdominal area and upper body and the shoulders. Use some oil to massage his penis and testicles (Carefully!) By doing this, you get him relaxed and excited, but also manage his experiences and how fast every little thing goes. You'll be warming him up and also unwinding him at the same time.

-Leave him Be

A final idea, strange maybe, is when he is having a split second where he's not thinking about sex, let him be! Snuggle, snuggle, and hug without any expectation of sex and you'll see that he'll get you more aroused than he ever would certainly have been if you would jump all over him. Even the horniest male needs time to charge, so by giving him this chance, you are showing respect and restraint, both of which will drive him wild when it's time for the main event again.

To have the best sex possible, you need to know that both companions need to be into it, and also, this indicates that your guy has been treated with the same foreplay respect as you would certainly like to be. Make sure you spend some time arousing him as well as you'll not only show your respect and love but also be rewarded by outstanding sex!

How to Be Sexy and also Irresistible to Men - Techniques to Make Him Fall For Your Charms

Technically talking, being attractive is something you can be any time of the day. Quit thinking that being alluring is something that you're birthed with or has usually and genetically refined itself to some lucky human beings. Being irresistible and sexy is a skill-- a handiness that can be learned and developed. Influences can be extremely handy, and a few lessons on self-worth and pictures can help you, but extra frequently than not, it can be through the power of the mind. So if you've been dwelling more about your instabilities and self problems, it's time to settle them up finally and get on a new goal-- below are the top ways on how to be tempting and sexy to men-- make him fall for your beauties at last!

-Get daring and playful. Non-verbal communication is exceptionally vital, specifically if it involves attraction and seduction. Subtlety can be incredible; that's why it pays to knows the right combination of signals to send to the opposite sex to make him go adventurous and flirt right back to you too.

-Attempt to feel and look good always. This regulation is extremely critical. Self-confidence is a need to if you desire to attract the male of your dreams. Well, technically, we're absolutely nothing without confidence. It is the very thing that makes us move on in life, love, and occupation. So start building yours.

-Learn how to tease his imagination. Don't do the what-you-see-is-what-you-get kind of attitude. Being alluring means you need to pique his interest and creativity. Make him get interested in you the more, and you are going to get him glued to you for as long as you want.

-Don't be also eager for attention. Be cool, girl—no need to be needy and desperate for his attention. Men love self-assured women, that have a life and will not do dumb things for a man's attention-- that is just too pitiful for words. So go on with your regimen (yet give in to impulses from time to time).

-Be an enigma. Do you want him to go back for more of you? Do not spill out every single feature of your life in a split second. It will kill the state of mind and would make you unexciting. Kick back and be more of a mystery-- he'll love that.

www.ingramcontent.com/pod-product-compliance
Lightning Source LLC
Chambersburg PA
CBHW050727030426
42336CB00012B/1440